DESPERATE

CROSSINGS

Books by Norman L. Zucker and Naomi Flink Zucker

The Guarded Gate: The Reality of American Refugee Policy (1987)
The Coming Crisis in Israel: Private Faith and Public Policy (1973)

Books by Norman L. Zucker

The American Party Process: Comments and Readings (1968)
George W. Norris: Gentle Knight of American Democracy (1966)

DESPERATE

CROSSINGS

SEEKING REFUGE IN AMERICA

NORMAN L. ZUCKER
NAOMI FLINK ZUCKER

M.E. Sharpe
Armonk, New York
London, England

Library of Congress Cataloging-in-Publication Data

Zucker, Norman L.
Desperate crossings : seeking refuge in America / Norman
L. Zucker, Naomi Flink Zucker
p.   cm.
Includes bibliographical references and index.
ISBN 1-56324-727-5 (alk. paper). —
ISBN 1-56324-728-3 (paperback : alk. paper)
1. Refugees—government policy—United States.
2. Asylum, Right of—United States.   3. United States—Emigration
and immigration.   I. Zucker, Naomi Flink.   II. Title.
JV6601.Z83   1996
362.87′0973—dc20   96-14378
CIP
Printed in the United States of America

The paper used in this publication meets the minimum requirements of
American National Standard for Information Sciences—
Permanence of Paper for Printed Library Materials,
ANSI Z 39.48-1984.

BM (c)   10   9   8   7   6   5   4   3   2   1
BM (p)   10   9   8   7   6   5   4   3   2   1

To Haras Harobed Rekcuz
and Leonard P.Q. Swineley,
who were there at the beginning.

Providing refuge to those facing persecution in their homeland . . . goes to the very heart of the principles and moral precepts upon which this country and its Constitution were founded. It is unavoidable that some burdens result from the protection of these principles. To let these same principles go unprotected would amount to nothing less than a sacrilege.

Nuñez v. Boldin

Contents

Acknowledgments

We began our research and writing on forced migration and refugees in 1980, in Washington, D.C., where Norman Zucker was a guest scholar at the Brookings Institution and a contributor-consultant to the Select Commission on Immigration and Refugee Policy. Three months after our arrival in Washington, the Refugee Act was signed, and, soon thereafter, the Mariel boatlift began. We observed and gathered data on both events, milestones in American refugee history. Over the last decade and a half, we have written a book, *The Guarded Gate: The Reality of American Refugee Policy,* as well as book chapters and articles on the subject of refugees. This book is an outgrowth of investigations that we began during the Mariel boatlift.

We have benefited from interviews with refugees, government officials, representatives of nongovernmental agencies, advocates, lawyers, and scholars. Many of these people began as colleagues and became our friends. Fellow scholars freely shared their unpublished materials, their ideas, their time, and their resources; we owe them an intellectual and personal debt.

We also were encouraged to use the facilities of the Centre for Refugee Studies, York University, Toronto, Canada; the Refugee Studies Programme of Oxford University, Oxford, England; the Berlin Institute for Comparative Social Research, Berlin, Germany; and the Harvard Law School Immigration and Refugee Program, Cambridge, Massachusetts. We profited from their resources and from the intellectual stimulation of their conferences. In Washington, D.C., the US Committee for Refugees and the Refugee Policy Group also shared their data with us.

Among the many who have helped us, the following people deserve particular thanks: Shara Abdulah, Howard Adelman, Belinda Allan, Deborah E. Anker, Robert L. Bach, Jochen Blaschke, Sharon Brown, Rolande Dorancy, John Evans, Steven Forester, Bill Frelick, Anne Fuller, Dennis Gallagher, Andreas Germershausen, Mark Gibney, Linda Gordon, Virginia Hamilton, Barbara E. Harrell-Bond, James C. Hathaway, Arthur C. Helton, Erwin A. Jaffe, Charles B. Keely, Harold Hongju Koh, Ira J. Kurzban, C. Michael Lanphier, Pamela H. Lewis, Cheryl Little, Gil Loescher, Jane Lowicki, Jocelyn McCalla, Hiram Ruiz, Julia A. Spinthourakis, Barry N. Stein, Dale F. (Rick) Swartz, Roger Zetter.

In tracking down the photographs, we were helped by Jerusalem Eyob, Virginia Hamilton, Betsy Lincoln, Darlene Pfluger, Eric Pumroy, brother Richard of Weston Priory, John Tenhula, and Marifrances Trivelli.

Gregg Beyer extended his help for many years and, in particular, carefully and critically read the manuscript.

Atle Grahl-Madsen and Jerry Tinker have died since we began our work, but we remain grateful for their friendship and help.

Margaret J. (Mimi) Keefe, Deborah Mongeau, Marie S. Rudd, and Michael C. Vocino, Jr., of the University of Rhode Island Library, handled our sometimes difficult requests with good humor and speed. Nicholas Ray was a conscientious and imaginative research assistant who cheerfully carried out a number of tasks.

We received from the University of Rhode Island Faculty Development Fund a number of grants for travel and research.

John T. Harney gave good counsel. Stephen J. Dalphin, our editor, understood from the start what we were trying to achieve and allowed us the (additional) time we needed.

As always, our children, Sara and Sam, gave us encouragement when we needed it, advice when we asked for it, and criticism whenever possible.

DESPERATE

CROSSINGS

Introduction: Crossings to America

For nearly fifty years, from the conclusion of the Second World War until the collapse of the Soviet Union, the world was divided into two camps, communist and non-communist. In geographic terms, the enemies were the East and the West, each fearing annihilation by the other. Today the Soviet Union is dead and communism an aged shadow, but a cold war of a different kind haunts us. The enemies now face off from north and south, and the threat is not annihilation, but invasion, invasion of the countries of the north by armies of migrants from the south. In this war, the armies of the north are border patrols and immigration authorities, the weapons restrictive laws, interdictions, "humane deterrence," and forced repatriations. Political leaders in the north appeal to patriotism and to fear, the fear of strangers crossing their borders. But the enemy is not a monolith; all migrants are not driven by the same needs, not drawn by the same prospects. Many of these migrants are refugees, people driven by fear of persecution and drawn by hope of safe haven.

It is the refugees' fear of persecution that forces them from home into the larger stream of migrants attempting to settle in another country. But their fear of persecution also separates them from other migrants, and it is this fear that, in receiving countries, both defines and protects them. Countries that are signatory to the Convention and Protocol relating to the Status of Refugees recognize as refugees those individuals with a "well-founded fear of persecution." Here is where the second characteristic of refugees—the hope of safe haven—separates them from other migrants. The convention and protocol require that individuals with a legitimate request for asylum be allowed to present their claims and that they not be returned to a country in which they fear persecution.

Increasingly, the refugee-receiving countries of Europe and North America are retreating from their obligations. As the numbers of both refugees and economic migrants rise, both are seen as unwanted burdens, as looming threats. Economic migrants and refugees alike are being barred from entry.

Plans are now being drawn up for a tunnel, under the Strait of Gibraltar, to link Spain and Morocco. While such a tunnel would ease trade and tourism between Europe and Africa, far-right groups in Europe are already predicting that the tunnel would also ease the movement of undocumented

Algerians, Moroccans, and Tunisians.[1] When, some years ago, a tunnel was proposed that would link England and France, there was also opposition, but the opposition did not raise fears of undocumented aliens. The difference lies in the opposing directions of the two tunnels—one east-west, the other north-south.

Tunnels ease the movement of people for commerce and pleasure; asylum laws in Europe were intended to ease the movement of refugees. But the refugees who benefited from those asylum laws were European refugees, refugees from Nazism and communism, refugees from the east. Asylum seekers today come from the south, and as they attempt to cross into the north, they are finding the barriers being raised.

It has been argued that the threat is not the *origins* of the asylum seekers, but their *numbers*. The numbers have grown enormously. In the decade before 1995, western Europe saw a tenfold increase in the number of people seeking asylum. But numbers are not the only, or even the primary, reason that both barriers and fears are being raised. In England, where the total number of asylum seekers is low, there was a backlash when Tamils began to apply for asylum. Winston Churchill, a Conservative member of Parliament and grandson of the wartime prime minister, in May of 1993, decried the "relentless flow" of immigrants, particularly those from the Indian subcontinent, warning that they threatened the British way of life and democracy.

Similarly in France, where there has been a slow but controlled increase in the numbers of asylum seekers, to fewer than 55,000 in 1990, Minister of the Interior Charles Pasqua became concerned that an insurrection in Algeria, if it intensified, would produce a stream of refugees in search of safety. He vowed to stop all immigration, saying, "France has been a country of immigration, but it no longer wishes to be."[2]

If France has not been overwhelmed by asylum seekers, the same is certainly not true for Germany, which, since 1989, has received nearly one million applicants for asylum. But France and Germany are linked in another way. After World War II, both countries enacted liberal policies toward refugees and asylum seekers, in part to absolve themselves of guilt for their wartime iniquities. In Germany's Basic Law of 1949, Article 16 grants the right to asylum to "persons persecuted for political reasons." But forty years later, while the numbers of asylum seekers in Germany had risen, the German economy had declined, and extremists found release for their frustrations in ugly attacks on foreigners. In 1993, the German Parliament amended its laws; although the right of asylum remains inviolate, a new article permits German authorities to turn back any asylum seeker who has traveled through a safe third country, a country that also offers asylum.

On its face, such an amendment appears benign. Why, after all, should a refugee travel through one safe country in order to reach another? The amendment is gaining wide approval in other countries, but the concept behind it is not benign. In reality, the responsibility for refugees would be transferred from economically developed, politically stable countries with established legal systems to developing, politically unstable countries with emerging legal systems. The countries that are most able to cope with the burden of refugees would place that burden on those countries that are least able.

In 1994, the United States included in its asylum regulations a similar provision, that an individual who is eligible for asylum could be denied asylum and deported to a country he or she had traveled through that was considered safe or where his or her asylum claim could be decided "in accordance with [an] arrangement with the United States."[3] The United States now has an agreement to that effect with Canada.

For the United States there has been a gradually increasing stream of migrants—both refugees and would-be immigrants—from the south, for more than thirty years. Neither the public nor government policy makers have responded to the problem with clarity or preparedness. Rather, entrants were assigned a status according to arbitrary criteria. For decades, foreign policy determined the status of entrants: If applicants came from communist countries, they were almost always determined to be refugees; if they came from non-communist countries, they were usually categorized as economic migrants.

The clearest example of this mindset is in the contrasting case histories of the Cuban and Haitian boat people. From the time that Castro rose to power, it became United States policy to admit virtually all Cubans who were able to leave Cuba. Conversely, Haitians who fled the brutal regimes of François Duvalier and his son Jean-Claude for the most part were denied asylum on the grounds that they were "economic migrants." Cubans rescued at sea by the Coast Guard were brought to the United States. But beginning in 1981, Haitians were interdicted at sea, in effect prevented from leaving Haiti. A similar contrast appears in the treatment of entrants from Central America. Nicaraguans, who fled a communist government, were welcomed in the United States and granted asylum. Guatemalans and Salvadorans, who fled the violence of right-wing governments, were, like the Haitians, interdicted, denied asylum, and deported.

Foreign policy remained the dominant consideration until the summer of 1980, when Cuban President Fidel Castro opened the port of Mariel. The stream of more than 130,000 fleeing Cubans was swelled by some 15,000 Haitians. By the time the Mariel crisis had ended, America's belief in the certitude of its refugee policy was shaken. It had become clear during the boatlift that, although Cubans, by virtue of coming from a communist country, had always been considered political refugees, *not* every Cuban who came during the boatlift had a well-founded fear of persecution. Conversely, State Department pronouncements aside, it was also clear that many of the Haitians who arrived during the same period *did* have such a fear.

Two other factors, long recessive, began to emerge: the numbers of refugees and the economic, social, and political costs of resettling them. After Mariel, the American public perceived both the numbers and the costs of refugees as too high, and there was vocal opposition, opposition that did not go unheeded by the Congress or the White House. But the clamorous voice of refugee restriction had not yet drowned the quiet voice of humanitarian concern. As the killings spread in El Salvador, Guatemala, and Nicaragua, refugees from those countries began moving northward. The United States government, maintaining its foreign policy position, denied asylum to Salvadorans and Guatemalans, while granting it to Nicaraguans. And the government now added to its arsenal of threats the threat of numbers, the warning that, if unchecked, floods of Central American refugees would breach our borders. But the American public did not respond as one. While many Americans did want to bar the door, others responded with compassion and assistance, offering sanctuary to undocumented Central Americans.

But in the competition between compassion and restrictionism, history and economics would eventually determine the winner to be restrictionism. As the civil wars in Central America subsided, so too did American compassion. Conversely, as American economic problems grew, so too did American restrictionism. By the summer of 1994, when the threat of another Mariel loomed, domestic fears had become predominant. Indeed, it could be argued that our invasion and occupation of Haiti—foreign policy decisions—were essentially motivated by the fears of the American public of large numbers of Haitian asylum seekers. The welcome mat had frayed. As wave after wave of *balseros* took to the sea, unhindered by Havana's police, the Clinton administration suddenly reversed a policy of more than thirty years and ordered that Cubans as well as Haitians were to be interdicted at sea, denied entry, and detained at the Guantanamo Naval Base. Moreover, Cubans now joined Haitians in detention.

More than just Cuban refugee policy had been altered. The entire basis for our refugee policy had shifted from foreign policy, a fixation on the overthrow of communism—to domestic policy, pressures from the voters to curtail the numbers of "illegal aliens" and to reduce the cost of government. There is a certain irony in the fact that domestic policy drove not only refugee policy but foreign policy as well. In order to placate an angry public, to prevent further "invasions" of Haitians, President Clinton ordered the invasion and subsequent occupation of Haiti. And, in an ironic reversal of our Cuban policy, the Clinton administration entered into negotiations with Fidel Castro to limit and regularize Cuban emigration to the United States. As a result, the Cuban refugee stream has been folded into an immigration quota.

Refugee policy in the United States has become an exercise in alchemy: how to transform refugees into immigrants, immigrants who can be controlled, regulated, and, above all, chosen. As in many other areas, America's actions become a bellwether for actions by the rest of the world. Case histories of the United States' response to Western Hemisphere refugees can stand as paradigms, not only for the United States, but for other refugee-receiving countries. The Cuban, Haitian, and Central American histories represent the full spectrum of American policy and practice toward refugees for nearly four decades. Even more important, these migrations all presage what future refugee movements are likely to be. In the future, foreign policy goals will probably not be the major determinant of refugee admissions. It is more probable that the converse will be true, that the prospect of refugee movements will become an influence on our foreign policy. And, in the future, our response to refugees is apt to be strongly influenced by demands to restrict and restrain the flow of refugees to our shores.

A refugee is someone with a "well-founded fear of persecution." Yet there are forces other than political persecution that drive people from their countries. Most of the Mariel Cubans, for example, had not been singled out for persecution yet felt unable to live with the restraints and hardships of Castro's government. Many Haitians were forced into flight by lawlessness and terror. Central Americans fled civil war and widespread violence. In each group, some would have been properly designated as refugees or granted political asylum, while others would not have fit these designations. Yet they had escaped their countries and reached ours in very large numbers. And for many, return to their own countries was impossible. They present a growing phenomenon, one that deserves urgent attention. We will call this phenomenon *mass escape* and these individuals *escapees*.

To regard mass escape movements as crises, and to respond to them as crises, is to disregard the past, ignore the present, and slight the future. The Caribbean and Central American exoduses have much to teach us about the causes, effects, and remedies of mass escape. First, United States refugee policy must depart from viewing sending countries in terms of their ideologies, whether of the left or of the right. Rather, refugee policy should examine the *human rights* conditions in these countries, since it is these conditions that produce escapees. Escapees are victims not of ideologies but of human rights abuses.

Further, our refugee policies have implications far beyond the escapees themselves or the receiving American communities. It was the threat of mass escapes from Haiti and Cuba that led to the invasion and occupation of Haiti and negotiations with Castro on immigration. Refugee policy now affects not only domestic policy, but foreign policy, international relations, and even questions of war and peace.

The United States, and the other countries of the north, must accept the perhaps unpalatable fact that in the post–Cold War world, there are now and will continue to be enormous increases in the numbers of people fleeing political repression, civil disorder, ecological disaster, and poverty. In the 1970s, when the United States was designing its refugee legislation, its first concern was for the refugees, people who were screened and processed outside the United States for permanent resettlement within the country. Asylum seekers, individuals who enter the country and ask for refuge, were only a secondary concern. In the 1980s, however, it became obvious that the question of asylum was pressing for attention and could not be ignored. Now, in the 1990s, the attention not only of the United States but of the entire refugee-receiving world has turned to the problem of mass escape.

In a sense, we have come full circle, since it was the mass refugee displacements of the Second World War that inspired the 1951 Convention relating to the Status of Refugees. In the years since, we have lost sight of what refugee protection was meant to achieve. It is a paradox of the times that international refugee and asylum protections are expanding while the nations of the world are constricting their immigration, refugee, and asylum laws. It is necessary now, fifty years after the war, to reclaim that early vision and bring it into the future.

Options for the future must be grounded in a clear understanding of the past. Chapter 1, "A Shifting Course: Immigrants," traces American immigration history, the alternation between welcome and rejection, between the admission and restriction of immigrants in response to the temperament of the times.

Although many of those who arrived in the United States had fled persecution, it was not until after the Second World War that these people were recognized as refugees, for whom a different standard and process of admission applied than were applied to immigrants. Chapter 2, "A Foreign-Policy Compass: Refugees and Asylum Seekers," analyzes the troika of interests that has influenced United States refugee policy.

A dominant influence on that policy came to be the mass escape movement that was the Mariel boatlift of 1980. Mariel was a watershed, an event that both defined the problem of mass flight and determined the American responses to it. Chapter 3, "The Mariel Floodtide: Mass Escape," shows that the boatlift itself was merely the culmination of decades of American policy. When the boatlift was stopped, however, the flood had left behind an ugly wreckage. The American public now perceived itself as helpless to withstand or even control the invasion of American shores by illegal entrants. The control of "illegal entrants" became a major political issue.

Politics was soon to become policy. After Mariel, that policy was to keep asylum seekers, as symbolized by the Haitian boat people, from reaching our borders. Chapter 4, "Erecting Floodgates: Escape by Sea," describes the measures—interdiction, deterrence, denial of due process—taken by the government to dissuade Haitians from seeking asylum and to deny to those who persisted fair and full hearings on their claims. These practices would be challenged in the courts, which upheld the legal rights of the refugees but did not alter either the practices of the government or the attitudes of the public.

Interdiction, deterrence, denial of due process were weapons the government continued to use against the Haitians. In chapter 5, "Erecting Fences: Escape Over Land," we will see those same weapons being used against Central Americans escaping from civil wars. But while formerly refugees had been welcomed because they fled the terrors of communist governments, the Salvadorans and Guatemalans were fleeing the terrors of governments that the United States supported. The escapees came, for many Americans, to symbolize their opposition to United States policy in Central America. For the first time, the escapees commanded the sympathy of large segments of the American people, and not only the courts but the Congress responded.

That sympathy would be short-lived. As the economy worsened, domestic fears and a rising tide of conservatism led to an upsurge of isolationism and xenophobia. Chapter 6, "In Foreign Waters: Barring Escape," depicts how Americans saw their worst fears realized with a second mass escape, in the summer of 1994, of Cubans and Haitians. The will of the American people to restrict and restrain immigration took control of our refugee policy. Indeed, so strong was this public pressure that refugee policy now determined foreign policy, directing the invasion of Haiti and the negotiations with Fidel Castro. Not only had the United States wrested control of our borders from Cuban and Haitian escapees, it had pushed those borders back to the shores of Cuba and Haiti.

But clearly, intervening militarily, as we have done in Haiti, must be a last, and seldom used, resort. Just as clearly, hindering escape from a repressive country, as we are doing in Cuba, does not further the cause of freedom. American refugee policy has been governed by shifting foreign policy imperatives, swayed by public pressures and prejudices. In recent years, unanticipated political upheavals have overturned all the previous foreign policy imperatives, leaving only public pressures and prejudices to dictate refugee policy. How can the United States and other countries of the north reconcile the competing demands of compassion and control? How is it possible to balance political utility with concern for human dignity? Chapter 7, "Charting a New Course," will suggest how in the future the United States and other refugee-receiving countries could prepare for and prevent future mass escapes, by means that can be both politically viable and compassionate. Although the challenge is formidable, it is possible to create a refugee regime that can respond effectively and humanely to future refugee flows.

1
A Shifting Course: Immigrants

From colonial times to the present, the United States has never been united in its attitudes toward newcomers. Admissionists have pressed for an open door, restrictionists a closed door. The late Barbara Jordan, as chair of the United States Commission on Immigration Reform, represented the admissionists when she wrote: "The United States has been and should continue to be a nation of immigrants. A well-regulated system of legal immigration is in our national interest." But Jordan also acknowledged, "There have always been those who despised the newcomers. The history of American immigration policy is full of racism and ethnic prejudice."[1]

Current American history is riddled with racism and ethnic prejudice. Patrick J. Buchanan, a sometime candidate for the Republican presidential nomination, summed up the restrictionist arguments:

> There are flood tides of new immigrants coming to the country and I think these . . . contribute to some of the social problems we've got in America. . . . If present trends hold, white Americans will be a minority in 2050 . . . our great cities are riven with gang wars among Asian, black and Hispanic youth who grow up to run ethnic crime cartels. . . . What happened to make America so vulgar and coarse, so uncivil and angry? Is it coincidence that racial and ethnic conflicts pervade our media when the racial and ethnic character of the US has changed more in four decades than in the previous twenty?[2]

Barbara Jordan exposed the prejudice behind the restrictionists' resentment. But resentment of immigrants flows from deeper springs than mere prejudice. Immigrants become, for many Americans, a safe target for their frustration with economic, social, even political problems. They argue that immigrants are taking American jobs, destroying American neighborhoods, demeaning American values. And the American government does nothing to stop the immigrants. The immigrant is a straw man, a spurious symbol for real frustrations. And a straw man is easily ignited on the bonfires of prejudice. This same straw man—the immigrant, or "the immigrant problem"—can also be the last best weapon of political opportunism. Politicians appealing to racial and ethnic prejudice can shield their diatribes behind the armor of patriotism.

Admissionists believe that immigrants and refugees substantially en-hance the well-being of the nation. By creating new jobs and paying taxes, they help expand the economy. They bring with them energy, skills, and intellectual capital. They enrich society with cultural and ethnic diversity and rejuvenate rather than retard a pluralistic nation. Immigrants cross the ocean to the United States, lured by the promise of opportunity in a new land; but many who in the past entered as "immigrants" were in actuality refugees, expelled from their homes by persecution and forced to find safe haven in another land. Admissionists take particular pride in what they see as America's humanitarian response to refugees. President Ronald Reagan expressed this ethos when he asked: "Can we doubt that only a divine Providence placed this land, this land of freedom, here as a refuge for all those people in the world who yearn to breathe free?"[3]

Restrictionists, on the other hand, believe that both immigrants and refu-gees diminish the nation. They steal jobs from Americans. They strain educational and health resources. And now they are accused of abusing the social security and welfare systems. They do not rejuvenate but retard the nation.

In the eighteenth century, the colonists objected to "jailbirds."[4] Benja-min Franklin inveighed against the Irish and the Germans. The Irish, he felt, echoing the popular view, were "a low and squalid class of people," while Germans were "clannish."[5] In 1797, when the population was not yet five million, Harrison G. Otis, of Massachusetts, argued, "When the country was new, it might have been good policy to admit foreigners. But it is so no longer."[6] The admissionist view was voiced by George Washington, who said that "the bosom of America is to receive not only the Opulent and respectable stranger, but also the oppressed and persecuted of all Nations and religions."[7]

Admissionists' arguments, buttressed by the real need to populate a vir-gin continent, kept the door open until after the Civil War. America needed foreigners more than it feared them. But the open door only fanned the flames of restrictionism. The Irish and Germans were the first waves of mass immigration. In the expanding frontier, they were settlers and labor-ers. In the industrializing cities, they ran the machines. But the Irish were Catholics. As the number of Catholics rose, so did the virulent anti-Catholic sentiment of the Native American party and the Know Nothing movement. The German Forty-Eighters, refugees from revolution, with their hostility to slavery and unorthodox political ideas, triggered another mode of nativism, a fear that immigrant radicals threatened established American institutions.

Both strains of nativism, religious bigotry and fear of foreign radicals, course through the immigration debate to the present. As the nation began to develop a federal immigration policy, the restrictionists' arguments began to make political inroads. Federal regulation of immigration, which originated in good intentions, within a decade had degenerated into noxious racial nativism. The first national legislation, the Immigration Act of 1875, banned prostitutes and convicts. From the reasonable exclusion of undesirables, it was a short step to Congress capitulating to racism.

Anti-Chinese sentiment incited the passage, in 1882, of the Chinese Exclusion Act. Most of the Chinese who had come to the United States were unskilled laborers who were willing to work hard for long hours and low wages. They had been recruited to lay railroad track and dig ore in the mines of the Southwest. But when the transcontinental railroad was completed, their labor was no longer needed. A depression in the 1870s ravaged the economy and incurred resentment against their continuing presence. Labor organizations protested foreign competition. Nativists protested the cultural and linguistic differences of the Chinese immigrants. Sinophobes held that the Chinese were unassimilable—criminals and prostitutes. The California Senate in 1876, in a frightening display of bigotry, resolved that the "Chinese are inferior to any race God ever made."[8] The exclusionary statute was not repealed until 1943. But this belated concession to our wartime ally was hollow. The statute was replaced by an invidious quota: Only 105 Chinese would be permitted entry annually. This quota remained in effect until 1965, when the era of immigration liberalization began.

Prejudice against the Chinese was embedded in law. But other immigrants also felt its lash. The second wave of mass immigration, which began in the 1880s, came primarily from southern and eastern Europe—Italians, Russians, Ukrainians, Slovaks, Poles, Croatians, Serbs, Magyars, Greeks, and Jews. The recession of 1893–97 impelled American restrictionists to rally against this new threat. In 1894, Boston bluebloods organized the Immigration Restriction League, which launched a campaign to alert the country to the social and economic dangers posed by the alien hordes. Edward A. Steiner, a professor at Grinnell College in Iowa, in a contemporary account, *The Immigrant Tide, Its Ebb and Flow,* described the hostility toward the new immigrants:

> Upon the immigrant the Boston man laid the blame for the degeneration of America and Americans.
> "What can you expect of our country with this scum of the earth coming in by the million? Black Hands, Socialists, and Anarchists? What can you expect?
> "The Sabbath is broken down by them as if it had never been a day of rest. They drink like fish, they live on nothing. . . ." He saw our country ruined, our flag in the dust, liberty dethroned and the Constitution of the United

States trampled under the feet of these infuriated Black Hands, Socialists and Anarchists.[9]

Pushed by the Immigration Restriction League, Congress passed a bill requiring a literacy test, but President Grover Cleveland vetoed the bill.

The pendulum swung toward the admissionists after the Spanish-American War reinvigorated the economy and spurred a need for unskilled immigrant labor. Once again, America needed foreigners more than it feared them. Two influential conservative business organizations, the Chamber of Commerce and the National Association of Manufacturers, came out against restrictionism. The desire for profit had temporarily triumphed over the desire for population purity.

Antiradical nativism rose up anew when anarchist Leon Czolgosz fatally shot President William McKinley. McKinley's successor, Theodore Roosevelt, recommended an educational test and urged Congress to bar "all persons who are anarchists . . . of low moral tendency or of unsavory reputation," as well as all "who are below a certain standard of economic fitness to enter our industrial field as competitors with American labor."[10] Congress responded with the Immigration Act of 1903. Although the act failed to impose a literacy test, it preserved American virtue by denying entrance to anarchists, beggars, and white slavers.

In 1907, immigration reached a peak. There was approximately one new immigrant for every sixty persons already in the United States. Southern and eastern European immigrants now outnumbered northern European immigrants by four to one. The numbers and the origins of the immigrants roused the restrictionists, who, in turn, convinced the Congress that the immigration imbalance was perilous. That year a joint Senate-House commission to study immigration was created and named for its chairman, Senator William Paul Dillingham of Vermont.

The Dillingham Commission labored and in 1911 produced a forty-two-volume report, a monument to insularity. The report, which affirmed the superiority of the Anglo-Saxon, mirrored the prejudices of the time: Immigrants from northern and western Europe were more desirable than immigrants from southern and eastern Europe. Southern and eastern European immigrants were criminally inclined, less skilled, more ignorant, and content with a lower standard of living. The commission concluded that immigration restriction was "demanded by economic, moral, and social considerations."[11] The door was closing. The report served as the rationale for the rigidly restrictive national-origins quota laws of the 1920s.

The era of immigration restriction would last for nearly half a century and began with the Immigration Act of 1917, a victory for the restrictionists. The act, passed over President Woodrow Wilson's veto on the eve of America's entry into World War I, contained four major provisions: literacy, an expanded list of deportables, Asiatic exclusion, and alien deportation.

Since the closing of the frontier, successive Congresses had battled presidents over the literacy test. Congresses had passed literacy test bills, but presidents Cleveland, Taft, and Wilson, in 1915, had vetoed them. In 1917, the literacy test finally became law. But to the dismay of the restrictionists, the literacy requirement (persons over sixteen had to be able to read thirty to forty words in some language) was not a significant barrier. A second provision added to the list of those already excluded persons of "constitutional psychopathic inferiority," men attempting to enter the country for immoral purposes, chronic alcoholics, stowaways, vagrants, and those with one or more attacks of insanity.[12]

A greater barrier was the exclusion of Asians. Chinese had earlier been barred by law. Japanese were kept out under a "Gentleman's Agreement" with Japan made in 1907 by Theodore Roosevelt. The act now extended those exclusions to all others coming from a huge geographical area designated as an Asiatic Barred Zone. (The restrictionists were less successful in excluding Africans. In 1915 an amendment was approved in the Senate to exclude from immigration "all members of the African or black race." But, after the NAACP mounted intense pressure, the House of Representatives defeated the proposal.[13])

The power to deport aliens who did enter the country, in a significant change from established practice, was expanded. In the nineteenth and early twentieth centuries deportation was a bureaucratic mechanism used to return recently admitted aliens who should have been denied admission at the port of entry. Under the new act, aliens who preached revolution or sabotage could be deported at any time after entry. The act, and subsequent legislation, raised deportation from a simple administrative procedure to a public policy weapon, a potent instrument for enforcing social, cultural, and political conformity.

The First World War fueled patriotism, conformity, and hostility to all things German. Speaking German was un-American. Sauerkraut was renamed "liberty cabbage." Dachshunds declined in popularity. These follies were but a prelude to the anti-immigration sentiment of the postwar decades.

Restrictionism reached its apogee in the 1920s, with an isolationism that caused the country to reject the Treaty of Versailles and the League of Nations. The decade was characterized by nativism, xenophobia, racial and ethnic prejudice, and bad scholarship in the guise of "scientific racism." The Russian Revolution nourished fears of foreigners and radicals, fears exacerbated by bomb scares and the devastating explosion outside J.P. Morgan and Company's Wall Street offices. Anarchists Nicola Sacco and Bartolomeo Vanzetti were tried and executed for murder. Attorney General A. Mitchell Palmer rounded up "radical" aliens and deported them. The Ku Klux Klan—antiblack, anti-Catholic, anti-Jew, and anti-immigrant—flourished. Unions, by contrast, lost members, causing union leaders to fear cheap immigrant labor.

Academics lent legitimacy to the concept of racial superiority. Madison Grant's *The Passing of the Great Race* and Henry Pratt Fairchild's *The Melting Pot Mistake* revealed their biases in their titles. Princeton psychologist Carl Brigham, after studying wartime army mental tests, concluded that Nordics were superior in intelligence to Alpine and Mediterranean people. Harvard's William MacDougall believed that Nordics possessed a self-assertiveness that had enabled them to dominate throughout history. Harry H. Laughlin, the expert for the House Immigration Committee, asserted, "The recent immigrants, on the whole, present a higher percentage of inborn socially inadequate qualities than do the older stocks."[14] All of these forces came together to urge that immigration be not merely restricted but stopped altogether.

Between 1919 and 1921, a spate of bills, all designed to close the door, was introduced in Congress. One bill proposed to suspend immigration for three years, another for four years, and still another for five years. These were modest suspensions when compared to the bill that proposed to prohibit immigration from Germany, Austria-Hungary, Bulgaria, Turkey, and their possessions for fifty years; immigration from other countries was to be prohibited for twenty years. The House of Representatives, bowing to the anti-immigration mood, passed a bill suspending all immigration for two years. The suspension never took effect, but stringent restriction was effected in the Quota Acts of 1921 and 1924. The era of immigration restriction had arrived.

The Quota Act of 1921 (the Johnson Act or First National Origins Act) was a watershed in American immigration history. The 1921 act limited European immigration from any country to 3 percent of what its foreign-born population had been in 1910, when 14.7 percent of the *total* population was foreign born.[15] But the restrictionists felt that even the 1921 law permitted the entrance of too many southern and eastern Europeans. The 1924 Johnson-Reed, or Second National Origins, Act was more draconian.

The Johnson-Reed Act retained the literacy test, the list of exclusions, and the list of nationalities barred, and it also reduced the annual admissible total. The annual quota for each nation was reduced to 2 percent of what that nationality had been in 1890. Moving the population base back twenty years reduced still further the numbers of southern and eastern Europeans.

The admissionists, a tiny minority from metropolitan districts that had large numbers of foreign born, argued that creating distinctions in admission categories would breed disunity in the American population. But the admissionist arguments were in vain.

The Immigration Act of 1924 grew out of two pervasive fears, fears that again hold sway today: fear of opening the floodgates to large numbers of newcomers and fear that those newcomers will threaten the existing social order. Kenneth Roberts, in a widely read series of articles in the mass-circulation *Saturday Evening Post,* wrote of European masses wanting to emigrate. Consular reports from southern and eastern Europe confirmed the prediction. The public saw hordes of foreigners threatening the public order, gangs of anarchists, bolsheviks, and criminals overrunning the country. Representative Albert Johnson, who gave his name to the act, declared that the American people

> have seen patent and plain, the encroachments of the foreign-born flood upon their own lives. They have come to realize that such a flood, affecting as it does every individual of whatever race or origin, cannot fail likewise to affect the institutions which have made and preserved American liberties. It is no wonder, therefore, that the myth of the melting pot has been discredited. It is no wonder that Americans everywhere are insisting that their land no longer shall offer free and unrestricted asylum to the rest of the world . . . the day of indiscriminate acceptance of all races, has definitely ended.[16]

The restrictionists had won. The 1924 act would set the direction of immigration policy for the next forty years, extending welcome to neither immigrants nor refugees.

As the United States was closing its doors to immigrants, Europe was being overspread with refugees. But the United States, isolationist and an ocean removed from the refugees, was not concerned with their protection. The violence accompanying the Soviet Revolution created over a million and a half refugees. Forced from their homes, stateless, and often penniless, these escapees were scattered throughout Europe and the Far East. Private charities, the Red Cross, and some governments provided temporary assistance. The escapees, however, unable or unwilling to return to their home countries, were in need not of temporary assistance but of permanent resettlement. Few of the refugees had identity papers; what papers did exist had been issued by the defunct tsarist government. Nor did the refugees have sufficient funds, and, without passports or money, they found themselves rejected almost everywhere. Some countries did issue temporary residency papers and allow the refugees to work, but when the temporary residency permits expired, the refugees were forced to depart and were frequently forbidden to return. Stateless persons became commonplace.

The refugee problem had grown widespread and burdensome, too wide-spread and burdensome a problem for private charitable organizations or even individual governments alone. The international community of states, through the League of Nations, recognized that it was obligated to protect refugees and find solutions to their problems. In 1921, the League institutionalized the first international refugee regime, creating the office of High Commissioner for Russian Refugees.

The first High Commissioner for Russian Refugees was the famous polar explorer Fridtjof Nansen of Norway. In the postwar years, when he worked out agreements to implement the repatriation of Russian, German, and Austro-Hungarian prisoners and internees, Nansen had established a reputation as a negotiator and a humanitarian. The League now turned to him to solve the problems caused by mass displacements of people in Europe and Asia Minor.

Nansen knew that a stateless person needed a legitimizing document, identification that would enable him to move between countries. And within a country an identity document would help the refugee to work and to obtain a residency permit. Nansen devised a certificate of identity, known as the "Nansen passport," which was issued by a host country. The passport was a poor substitute for a nation's own document. It was valid for only one year, it was renewed at the discretion of the issuing country, and the issuing country could refuse the refugee the right to return to that country. Nonetheless, with the passport, the refugee had the protection of the High Commissioner's Office. The Nansen passport, Dennis Gallagher of the Refugee Policy Group has noted, "became an early tangible symbol of the international community's responsibility for the legal protection of refugees."[17]

While Nansen was trying to assist the Russian refugees, Armenians who fled Turkish persecution also became refugees in need of protection. Armenians were made eligible for Nansen passports in 1924. But a passport does not provide resettlement. Nansen had difficulty resettling the Armenians. The United States had closed its doors. The Latin American countries, like the United States, were unwilling, even for refugees, to relax their stringent immigration laws.

As the refugee crisis continued, the world was caught in a worsening depression. Unemployment was deep and widespread in Europe and in the United States. In March 1933, Adolph Hitler assumed dictatorial powers in Germany and incited an outpouring of Jews and antifascists. The Anschluss (the incorporation of Austria into Germany), the annexation of the Sudeten-land, the occupation of Czechoslovakia, and the invasion of Poland and with it the beginning of World War II, swelled the refugee tide.

The League, in 1933, responded to refugee flows by establishing the office of High Commissioner for Refugees coming from Germany and by promulgating the Convention relating to the International Status of Refugees. The office of the High Commissioner for German Refugees proved to be ineffective, but it served as a model for the subsequent establishment of the United Nations High Commissioner for Refugees.[18] The convention, while it had only a very limited effect, was an important first step toward creating an international refugee regime.[19] Refugees were recognized to have specific rights. The most crucial of these was the prohibition against *refoulement.* No refugee could be forcibly returned to a country in which she or he had suffered or would be subject to persecution.

But the nascent international regime could not compel any country to admit refugees. In the words of Chaim Weizmann, for refugees the world was "divided into places where they cannot live and places into which they cannot enter."[20] This was the crux of the refugee problem: For refugees there was no safe haven.

For refugees around the globe it was the era of barred doors. Only Shanghai's International Settlement was hospitable.The United States would not be invaded by European refugees and would make no distinction between voluntary migrants seeking opportunity and forced migrants fleeing persecution.

An attempt to find safe haven for political refugees was made in the summer of 1938 at Evian-les-Bains, France. The Evian Conference, called at the suggestion of President Franklin D. Roosevelt, had wide participation. But this wide participation came about, Alan Dowty wrote in *Closed Borders: The Contemporary Assault on Freedom of Movement,* "only by promising that no nation would be asked to accept additional immigrants." Professor Dowty suggests that "the principal aim in promoting the conference was precisely to head off any pressure to increase American quotas."[21] The only concrete measure taken at the conference was the establishment of the Intergovernmental Committee on Refugees, which, with its secretariat in London, remained in existence until 1947.

In the United States, the doors of admission were held shut by many bars. The bar of the Depression with its massive unemployment. The bar of social and economic breakdown. The bar of nativism. The bar of anti-Semitism. The bar of isolationism. No efforts by refugee advocates could break down those bars. The doors remained shut. From 1933 through 1938, Congress chose to ignore a variety of bills on behalf of refugees. Only the Wagner-Rogers bill received serious attention.

The Wagner-Rogers bill was the quintessential confrontation between the admissionists and the restrictionists. But this time the issue was not immigration in general but the specific admission of refugee children. The bill proposed the admission, in 1939, on a nonquota basis, of 10,000 German children under fourteen and another 10,000 in 1940. In an attempt to soften the prevalent strong anti-Semitism, the bill was deliberately termed a German, rather than a Jewish, refugee children's bill. The public committee to support the bill was also deliberately called the Non-Sectarian Committee for German Refugee Children. At hearings on the bill, in April and May of 1939, when it was already clear that Jews in Germany were being persecuted, few American Jews testified. Clarence Pickett, the executive secretary of the American Friends Service Committee and chairman of the Non-Sectarian Committee, testified that the proposed legislation dealt with "children of all faiths."

The cause was clearly humanitarian, and there was an outpouring of support from pillars of the Christian establishment. Many were in favor of the legislation: Mrs. Calvin Coolidge, whose husband had signed the Johnson-Reed Act; former president Herbert Hoover, who had once stated his position as "strongly in favor of restricted and selected immigration";[22] former Republican presidential candidate Alf Landon; and nationally known Kansas journalist William Allen White. The list of prominent supporters was joined by a variety of prestigious religious and sectarian organizations: the Federal Council of Churches of Christ in America, the American Unitarian Association, the National YMCA, the Methodist Federation for Social Service, and the executive of the Boy Scouts of America. And the traditionally anti-immigrant AFL and the CIO, in an about-face, supported the bill.

But the humanitarian appeals fell before the onslaught of nativism and anti-Semitism. John B. Trevor of the American Coalition of Patriotic Societies called for a protest to Congress "to protect the youth of America from this foreign invasion." Mrs. James H. Houghteling, the wife of the commissioner of immigration, ominously warned that "twenty thousand charming children would all too soon grow up into twenty thousand ugly adults." The Grand Army of the Republic's national legislative chairman opined that it was impossible to "Americanize" any immigrant over the age of four. The Daughters of the American Revolution, the American Legion, and other numerically strong patriotic groups also opposed the children's bill.[23]

The opponents of the bill had a strong base. Two-thirds of the American public sampled in a Gallup poll believed that refugee children should not be admitted. Senator Robert F. Wagner, a liberal democrat from New York, was swamped with hate mail. His colleague, Senator Robert R. Reynolds, a restrictionist from North Carolina, on the other hand, was cheered for his bill, which would have suspended all immigration indefinitely. And another bill proposed that "every alien in the United States shall be forthwith deported."[24]

Despite its nonsectarian title, the public recognized that the modest bill was intended for the rescue of Jewish children. Official Washington understood the public. The State Department opposed the bill. The Department of Labor waffled. The White House was silent. In the end, political pragmatism won out over unbiased morality. The refugee children bill failed. One year later, Congress, with alacrity, passed a bill to allow the entrance of British children. President Roosevelt's silence on the children's bill, certainly a moral omission, probably could be rationalized by domestic politics. He was having trouble with the isolationists in Congress, the economy was still weak, anti-immigrant and anti-Jewish sentiments were high. There would be no political gain in alienating large segments of the voting public.

The State Department, during the era of barred doors, pursued a clear antirefugee policy. In the first week of June 1939, on the eve of Hitler's invasion of Poland, the SS *St. Louis,* carrying 937 Jews who believed they had bought valid visas to enter Cuba, sailed for Havana. But they were not permitted to dock there. The *St. Louis* sailed on to American waters, but now they were prevented from docking in Miami, Florida. An American Coast Guard cutter patrolled the coast to prevent any of the escapees from reaching shore. The desperate passengers sent two telegrams to President Roosevelt but received no response. The State Department, not wanting to set a precedent, refused to permit anyone not holding a valid visa to land. The ship, with all of its hopeless passengers, returned to Europe. Not one American newspaper spoke out on behalf of admitting the refugees.[25]

Perhaps if public sentiment had been inclined to accept refugees, official Washington might have acted differently. But Washington mirrored the country's restrictionist posture. Congress maintained existing bars to entry by refusing to pass legislation to admit refugees. The Department of State deliberately created new bars to exclude refugees.

The Department of State constructed, in historian David S. Wyman's memorable term, "paper walls," imposing ever stricter administrative requirements. It was no longer sufficient for relatives to furnish affidavits of financial support; there must also be evidence that the ship passage had been paid. During the critical years from 1940 to 1944, Assistant Secretary of State Breckenridge Long was primarily responsible for refugee matters. Long, a restrictionist and an admirer of Mussolini, spelled out his methods in a memorandum:

> We can delay and effectively stop for a temporary period of indefinite length the number of immigrants into the United States. We could do this by simply

advising our consuls to put every obstacle in the way and to require additional evidence and to resort to various administrative devises which would postpone the granting of visas.[26]

The State Department bureaucracy did "delay and effectively stop" refugees applying for safe haven. Under Long, a restrictionist policy was implemented by administrative fiat. Regulation was piled on top of regulation. A "relatives rule" stipulated that any visa applicant with a close relative remaining in German, Italian, or Russian territory had to pass a security test. This rule was subsequently broadened to require that all immigrant applications undergo a security review by a special interdepartmental committee. Papers moved with a slowness painful even for a bureaucracy. "Even when an applicant faced immediate danger," Professor Wyman has observed, "the State Department would not expedite the case."[27] By July 1943, when the Final Solution was well under way, the visa application form was more than four feet long and had to be filled out on both sides and submitted in sextuplicate. Long saw the refugees as "immigrants" to be kept out, his prejudice blinding him to their being victims of persecution, not masters of opportunity.

Policy making by administrative regulation can block or it can benefit. During the Second World War, policy was used to block the admission of refugees, to assure that the doors would remain barred. If there had been political will, administrative discretion just as easily could have been used to benefit the refugees. Much could have been done without violating or changing existing law. FDR made very modest inroads in restrictionist policy when he softened the "likely to become a public charge" clause and when he ordered the extension of German visitors' visas. (The "likely to become a public charge" clause was included in the restrictive Immigration Law of 1917, a vague phrase that left much to the discretion of an American consul. The clause was intended to keep out persons unable to support themselves who would become dependent on the public purse.) Businessmen could have been permitted entrance under the Treaty-Merchant provision of the immigration law. Temporary immigrants might have been settled in the Virgin Islands. Greater use could have been made of visas for visitors, clergymen, and academics. Children could have been exempted from quotas. And "temporary havens" or "free ports" could have been created.[28] (When the idea of free ports came up, Secretary of War Henry L. Stimson cautioned against "inundations by foreign racial stock out of proportion to what exists here."[29]) The United States did create a free port, Fort Ontario in Oswego, New York, but it received fewer than a thousand people.

The lack of distinction between an immigrant and a refugee and the concerted attempt to bar refugees from the United States did not represent a policy failure. Sadly, the policy was a success; policy makers who reflected the current ethos attained their goals. In retrospect, however, the policy was clearly a moral failure. It remained for President Harry S. Truman to try to reverse restrictionist policy and urge that refugees be admitted. The Truman years saw the beginnings of the second international refugee regime and ushered in, for the United States, a new period of refugee policy.

2
A Foreign-Policy Compass: Refugees and Asylum Seekers

United States' immigration policy from colonial times to the beginning of World War II was relatively uncomplicated. To both public and policy makers all migrants were "immigrants" to be admitted or denied entrance. But the Russian Revolution and the rise of militant fascism in Germany and Italy rudely thrust the forced migrant onto the world's consciousness. These migrants, who had been driven out of their homelands, were refugees; they were, in a crucial sense, different from would-be immigrants seeking opportunity in new homelands. This critical difference—the difference between those who are *forced* to migrate and those who *choose* to migrate—was not then recognized. But with the surrender of Hitler's military, refugees, a phenomenon as old as human misery, were given a new name: displaced persons (DPs). DPs were the survivors of the Holocaust and others, expelled from or forced to flee their homelands, who could not return.

For most of American history, the era of immigration, the law had made no distinction between a refugee and an immigrant. That distinction would be made for the first time during the Truman administration, when Congress passed the Displaced Persons Act of 1948. Ignoring the restrictionists, Harry S. Truman issued a presidential directive that eased the immigration of DPs to the United States under existing quotas. (The Fort Ontario internees were the first beneficiaries of the directive.) As the directive brought in only a small number (from the spring of 1946 through June of 1948 some 40,000 DPs were issued visas),[1] Truman asked Congress for special legislation to admit DPs outside the existing immigration quotas. The political stage was now set for the first postwar policy battle between the restrictionists and admissionists.

This, however, was not to be the usual immigration debate. The debate was not over immigrants but over displaced persons. The world now knew the truth of Nazi inhumanity and knew as well that beyond the barred doors millions had been incarcerated, dehumanized, and killed. But as Gil Loescher and John A. Scanlan point out in *Calculated Kindness: Refugees and America's Half-Open Door, 1945 to the Present,* "Traditional restrictionist attitudes remained potent in Congress, and ... considerable anti-Semitism existed both on Capital Hill and in the populace at large."[2] American admissionists might feel remorse, but alone they could not muster the strength to unbar the gates. The admissionists had first to disarm the arguments of the restrictionists.

Spearheading the drive to counter the restrictionists was a well-organized lobbying group, the Citizens' Committee on Displaced Persons (CCDP). The CCDP crafted a campaign that subordinated humanitarian and moral obligations to the more practical concerns of a broad constituency. The economic benefits of DPs were stressed: The unemployment rate was very low, and the strong postwar economy needed agricultural workers and skilled laborers. The CCDP succeeded in convincing labor unions and the American Legion, both traditionally opposed to immigration, that the DP legislation was not a threat. And overlaying all the arguments for and against admission, which were based on purely domestic concerns, there was also concern over foreign policy.

The Cold War had begun, and it suffused the DP legislation with its politics. The DP bill embraced not only survivors of the Holocaust, but also persons from areas that the Soviet Union had annexed. As initially passed, the DP Act "was fraught with restrictions and appeared purposely designed to favor groups other than surviving European Jews."[3] To be eligible for admission to the United States, a DP had to have been in Germany before December 22, 1945, the date of Truman's original presidential directive. The practical effect of this cutoff was to make ineligible the Jewish survivors of concentration camps who had fled to the west after the Polish pogroms of 1946. The bill also gave priority for admission to other categories of DPs such as Balts and those involved in agriculture, further reducing the numbers available to Jews.

The DP Act replaced the Truman directive, and to ensure that the immigration laws would not be changed, it proposed to admit 100,000 DPs under mortgaged quotas. Under the quota system, if all visas for the current year were taken, half of the visas for future years could be mortgaged, used by the DPs but not available for later immigrants from the same country. The results were ludicrous. By 1951 the Lithuanian quota had been mortgaged to the year 2079, the Estonian to 2130, and the Latvian to 2255. President Truman reluctantly signed the Displaced Persons Act in June of 1948, the same month the Berlin blockade began.

Some of the Balts who were beneficiaries of the DP Act were the first "boat people" to cross the ocean after World War II. Some 30,000 escapees, Estonians, Latvians, and Lithuanians, had sailed to Sweden after the Soviet takeover of their homelands. When it appeared that the Swedish government would comply with the Russian request to return them to their countries, many of the escapees took to the sea in small boats. The first of these boats, the *Erma,* arrived in Little Creek, Virginia, on December 15, 1945. Sixteen Estonians, men, women, and children, had survived an 8,000-mile, 128-day voyage in a 37-foot sloop. Other boats followed. But on reaching shore, the escapees were put into deportation proceedings. After urgings by Truman, Congress enacted legislation giving the Balts the status of DPs and making them eligible for permanent admission and ultimate naturalization.[4]

The Displaced Persons Act, despite having been watered down by the restrictionists, was the first significant refugee legislation in American history. Congress, in mortgaging future quotas, had recognized that refugee numbers might not be contained within normal immigration quotas. The act was liberalized by amendment in 1950 and extended in 1951. Over 400,000 DPs found homes in the United States. Although the restrictionists had written their biases into the law, the Displaced Persons Commission that administered the act did so liberally. Unlike the State Department bureaucracy, which had been restrictionist in the 1930s and early 1940s, the DP Commission bureaucracy was admissionist.

A troika of interests—foreign policy, the costs of resettlement, and domestic pressures—had shaped the passage of the DP Act. This troika dominated refugee decisions from the Cold War period to the present. This is not an amicable troika, in which the three horses trot in harness toward the same goal. Indeed, this would hardly seem to be a team at all, since two of its members want to move in opposing directions and the third is constantly shifting, moving first with one and then with the other. Ultimately, refugee policy is driven by this troika of interests.

The first member of the team, foreign policy, usually the strongest, has a clear intention and a momentum—to bar from or admit to the United States specific refugee groups that further its goals. An anticommunist foreign policy urged the admission of persons fleeing Iron Curtain countries, Indochina, Cuba, and Nicaragua. Conversely, it urged the barring of Haitians, Guatemalans, and Salvadorans.

The second member of the team, costs of resettlement, also has a firm goal—to restrict the numbers of refugees admitted and restrain the budget of domestic refugee programs. Traditionally, budgetary considerations have been the weakest member of the troika.

The third member of the team, domestic pressures, vacillates, shifting its direction from admission to restriction depending on the interplay of forces holding its reins. When lobby groups are united and are in accord with a given foreign policy, the result is clear. Jewish pressure groups were successful in gaining refugee status for Soviet Jews. Cuban lobbies were successful in gaining the entrance of Cubans. Armenians in the United States were ambivalent about pushing for the admission of Soviet Armenians, and admission policies reflected that ambivalence.

While the troika of interests in the United States was struggling to fashion the DP Act, the United Nations' successor to the League of Nations, was grappling with the problem of postwar Europe's DPs and refugees. Toward the end of 1946, the General Assembly created the International Refugee Organization (IRO). Initially conceived as a temporary repatriation agency, under the pressures of the Cold War the IRO became a resettlement vehicle for those who had "valid objections" to returning home to the east bloc.[5] The IRO, working cooperatively with voluntary agencies, resettled over a million Europeans between 1947 and 1951.[6]

The IRO was succeeded by the United Nations High Commissioner for Refugees (UNHCR), which would become one of two pillars of the second international refugee regime. The UNHCR was originally given a three-year mandate to provide international protection and seek permanent solutions to refugee problems. This mandate has been renewed for successive five-year terms, and the UNHCR is the center of the present transnational refugee structure. But the office is severely circumscribed by the constraints of international and domestic politics.

The other pillar of the second international refugee regime is the UN Convention relating to the Status of Refugees. The convention, a milestone in international law, is a multilateral treaty that enumerates the obligations of signatory states to refugees. Central to the convention are its definitions of a refugee and of nonrefoulement.

The convention definition superseded the League's definition, which was tied to specific national groups. A convention refugee was a person who:

> as a result of events occurring before 1 January 1951 and owing to a well-founded fear of being persecuted for reasons of race, religion, nationality, membership of a particular social group or political opinion, is outside the country of his nationality and is unable or, owing to such fear, is unwilling to avail himself of the protection of that country; or who, not having a nationality and being outside the country of his former habitual residence as a result of such events, is unable or, owing to such fear, is unwilling to return to it.[7]

The articulation of nonrefoulement was simple and direct:

> No contracting State shall expel or return ("refouler") a refugee in any manner whatsoever to the frontiers of territories where his life or freedom would be threatened on account of his race, religion, nationality, membership of a particular social group or political opinion.

While the principle of nonrefoulement protects refugees, it does not afford them asylum. It is the right of receiving governments to grant or to deny asylum.[8] The 1948 Universal Declaration of Human Rights provided only the right to *seek* asylum. The 1951 convention went no further.

The convention also set standards for the treatment of refugees in important areas such as legal status, employment, and welfare. But it was limited in time and geography; it applied only to persons who became refugees before January 1, 1951, and signatory states could limit its extent to Europe. In contrast, the UNHCR was given competence to deal with refugees irrespective of when they became refugees or where they were. In 1967, the Protocol relating to the Status of Refugees removed the limitations of the 1951 convention. The United States never acceded to the 1951 convention but became a signatory to the 1967 protocol, accepting in theory the universalist principles of the refugee regime.

But in practice, United States refugee policy never became universalist. Anticommunism became the foundation of American foreign policy. Refugee policy was made to serve the larger foreign policy goals of undermining eastern bloc communism. Refugee-escapees who fled to the West were "voting with their feet"; defectors proved the inadequacies of the communist system.

Anticommunist passions would prove so strong that they began to make inroads into American restrictionism, a restrictionism embedded in the major immigration legislation of the 1950s, the McCarran-Walter Act. The McCarran-Walter Immigration Nationality Act of 1952 retained the national-origins quota system, but, in a faint gesture to internationalism, repealed the exclusion of the Japanese and other Asians. The gesture, however, was no more than a hint. The Chinese quota of 105 was retained, Japan was given a quota of 185, and countries in the Asia-Pacific Triangle were each given a quota of 100.[9] Another provision, however, presaged important future changes. The act authorized the attorney general to parole, or admit, aliens into the United States temporarily. The parole provision, intended to be applied case by case, was subsequently used to circumvent the immigration laws and admit groups of refugees.

European refugees from communist countries soon breached the McCarran-Walter Act. Urged by presidents Truman and Eisenhower, Congress abandoned the numerical limits and quotas for refugees from communism, even allocating funds for their assistance. The President's Escapee Program (PEP), begun in 1952, was followed by the Refugee Relief Act (RRA) a year later. The RRA, further relaxing immigration law, authorized more than 200,000 nonquota visas for persons escaping from Iron Curtain countries.

Just as the RRA was about to expire, the Hungarian uprising began, and thousands of "freedom fighters" fled to Austria. The Hungarians were the first escapees to be admitted en masse into the United States. Some were given visas under the RRA; others, at Eisenhower's direction, were admitted under a new and decidedly elastic interpretation of the parole provision. This was the first use of parole on behalf of a group of refugees, and it became the legal basis for the admission of other refugee groups.

Still other Hungarians were admitted under the Refugee-Escapee Act (REA) of 1957. The REA was significant in two ways. First, in a shift in the immigration law, the act repealed the existing mortgages against quotas. Second, the REA defined refugee-escapees as victims of communist-occupied or communist-dominated countries or a country in the Middle East. This narrow definition remained American law until 1980, when the more universalist definition of the protocol was incorporated into the Refugee Act.

Hungarian resettlement succeeded for several reasons. The number of escapees who came to the United States was small, slightly more than 38,000 out of over 171,000. (The remainder went to some thirty other countries that, in a reversal of their prewar policies, now opened their doors to the refugees.)[10] The Hungarians had a well-established ethnic community in the United States to cushion their arrival. Unemployment was low. They were white Europeans who were highly employable. They had few dependents. And finally, they were anticommunists whose brave stance made them worthy adornments to American democracy.[11]

Two elements of the troika—foreign policy interests and domestic pressure—also urged the admission of groups in the Western Hemisphere. The Hungarian stream was ending, but in the neighboring Caribbean, political changes were occurring. In 1957, François ("Papa Doc") Duvalier was elected president of Haiti. In January 1959, Fidel Castro seized power in Cuba. The accession to power of these two dictators precipitated several decades of Cuban and Haitian mass escape to the United States. In Cuba, only ninety miles from Florida, Fidel Castro had overthrown Fulgencio Batista's corrupt government and installed a communist government. In analyzing Castro's takeover, Cuban-American historian Félix R. Masud-Piloto has concluded: "The United States' main concern in Cuba, however, was less the legality of the government than the ideology of its leaders. Communism, communist influence, and American economic interests were the real issues."[12]

Washington and Havana soon took actions that hardened mutual antagonisms. Castro promised elections but never held them. He did not reinstate the Cuban constitution. After summary trials, and despite vigorous protests from the Eisenhower administration, many of Batista's officials were executed. The Land Reform Law expropriated large tracts of land, some owned by Americans.

The economic war escalated. As Washington curtailed American trade with Cuba, Cuba signed a trade agreement with the Soviet Union. When, in April 1960, Soviet oil began to arrive, at Washington's behest American and British refineries refused to process it. Washington cut Cuba's sugar quota, but Moscow promised to purchase Castro's unsold sugar. In October 1960, Cuba nationalized most US businesses. In January 1961, Havana demanded that the US embassy, within forty-eight hours, reduce its staff to eleven. The next day, Eisenhower severed diplomatic and consular relations. In February 1962, the United States imposed a trade embargo on Cuba.

Paralleling the economic clashes were a series of military threats. In April 1961, Cuban exiles, advised, trained, and equipped by the CIA, invaded the island's Bay of Pigs. Castro's forces quickly routed and imprisoned the invaders. In the fall of 1962 came the Cuban Missile Crisis.[13] Along with the overt military threats, there was also covert conduct. "Eisenhower," analyst George Black wrote, "had decided that Washington could no longer coexist with Castro, and he authorized a program of covert actions to get rid of the Cuban leader. Over the next several years, the CIA would attempt to assassinate Castro with exploding cigars and poisoned milkshakes, and humiliate him with depilatory powders that would make his beard fall out."[14] But all attempts to dislodge or outwit Castro failed. There remained but one way to embarrass Castro and point up the shortcomings of Cuban communism: Cubans fleeing to the United States would be welcomed as refugees from political repression, lauded as risking all for freedom.

Castro's escapees, in addition to receiving a warm welcome, also received material assistance. By November 1960, Cuban refugees were flooding into Florida at the rate of 1,700 a week. Like other refugees before them, they had had to leave their assets behind. At first, voluntary agencies responded to the emergency with private resources. Then, in December 1960, Eisenhower established the Cuban Refugee Center in Miami and gave the voluntary agencies federal funds to aid in resettlement. The United States was now a country of first asylum for a large number of refugees, and the federal government assumed significant financial responsibility for their resettlement.[15] Foreign policy, abetted by pressure groups (Cuban-Americans, state and local officials, resettlement organizations) had triumphed over frugality. Resettlement costs were a small price to pay to embarrass and weaken Castro.

From the Castro revolution until 1961, when the United States broke off relations with Cuba and stopped all commercial flights, Cubans came directly to Florida; they benefited from an extraordinarily liberal nonimmigrant visa policy in Havana and a pro forma grant of political asylum in the United States. From 1961, when the direct flights were ended, until 1965, Cubans went first to third countries, where they were given parole visas for the United States. One exception was made in May and June of 1963. After the Bay of Pigs invasion, the United States paid a ransom for the return of the invaders. When the ships that carried the ransom to Cuba returned to the United States, they carried Cuban political prisoners and their families.[16]

During the early 1960s when Cubans were entering the United States, the Kennedy administration was developing refugee legislation that made the emergency Cuban program permanent. (The Cuban Refugee Program remained in existence until it was phased out in October 1981 by the Refugee Act of 1980.) The Kennedy administration sought to lessen the restrictions on immigration while at the same time making permanent America's commitment to refugees abroad. The Migration and Refugee Assistance Act (MRAA), enacted in 1962 to extend indefinitely the earlier Refugee Fair Share Law, was the first comprehensive refugee assistance statute. It remained the basic refugee law until superseded by the Refugee Act. It gave the executive a broad, permanent, and flexible mandate to conduct refugee affairs. The MRAA supported assistance programs for refugees and escapees. And, recognizing the role of the second international refugee regime, it provided for annual contributions to the UNHCR and the Intergovernmental Committee for European Migration (now the International Organization for Migration).

Just before the MRAA became law, a refugee emergency arose in Hong Kong. Communist China temporarily relaxed its border controls, and Chinese began pouring into Hong Kong. Seeing an opportunity to act against communism, Kennedy announced that, under the parole provision, he would admit several thousand Chinese to the United States. But his action served more to unify families than to aid refugees: the Chinese admitted were not the Chinese who had just fled, but those who had been cleared for immigration to the United States since 1954 but had been unable to enter because of the tiny Chinese quota. However, the administration's willingness to admit several thousand Chinese presaged a more liberal policy toward Asians.

In the third year of his presidency, JFK submitted legislation that, if enacted, would have liberalized immigration policy. Kennedy wanted to give the executive power to admit refugees, to abolish the racist Asian-Pacific Triangle, and, over a five-year transition period, to eliminate the national-origins quota system. But Kennedy's assassination brought a temporary halt to immigration reform.

Under Kennedy's successor, Lyndon B. Johnson, the country's mood was liberal. The legislation that emerged from the Congress, the Immigration Act of 1965, signaled the beginning of the era of liberalization. The 1965 act abolished the national-origins quota system and the Asian-Pacific Triangle, and in so doing, radically altered the ethnic balance of future immigration. With the passage of the act, the weight of immigration shifted from Europe to Asia and Latin America, a shift that would impel renewed restrictionism in the 1990s. Under the act, 170,000 Eastern Hemisphere immigrants would enter each year, and only 120,000 from the Western Hemisphere. An Eastern Hemisphere preference system was established, giving priorities on a scale of one through six for family ties and occupational skills. No preference system was created for the Western Hemisphere until 1976. In 1978, President Jimmy Carter signed a bill that combined the two hemispheres into a single preference system and a worldwide ceiling of 290,000.

The Immigration Act of 1965 also specifically addressed the needs of refugees. Congress placed refugees seventh—last—in Eastern Hemisphere preferences and gave them the smallest 6 percent, or 10,200—of all entrants. (When the Western Hemisphere was brought into the preference system, the number of refugees eligible for admission was raised to 17,400.) But in the refugee policy Congress wrote into law, refugees were ancillary to immigration and subject to geographic, ideological, and numerical restrictions. A refugee continued to be defined as an individual fleeing racial, religious, or political persecution from any communist, communist-dominated, or Middle Eastern country. Congress also specifically rejected the use of the parole provision for mass admissions.

But even before the act was signed, President Johnson was forced to ignore Congress's prohibition against using the mass paroles. The Cuban economy, fettered by US sanctions, had deteriorated badly, causing considerable dissension, particularly among the middle classes.[17] For Fidel Castro, one way to rid Cuba of dissidents was to permit them to emigrate. Direct emigration to the United States had been terminated after the missile crisis, and the number of Cubans relocating to the United States via third countries had dropped to an average of only 35,000 annually. Suddenly, on September 28, 1965, Castro announced to a large gathering in Havana's Plaza de la Revolucion that Cubans whose American relatives requested it would be allowed to leave, beginning on October 10, from the small port of Camarioca. In Washington, the State Department was taken by surprise and issued its stock response that American "policy always has been to admit bona fide refugees from communist aggression."[18] A week later, on October 3, President Johnson signed the Immigration and Nationality Act of

1965 at the Statue of Liberty and proclaimed an open-door policy for Cubans: "I declare this afternoon to the people of Cuba that those who seek refuge here in America will find it. The dedication of America to our tradition as an asylum for the oppressed is going to be upheld."[19]

Doors had been opened both in Cuba and in the United States, and a massive migration crisis was in the making. A second wave of Cubans was about to arrive on Florida's shores. Hundreds of boats, of all sizes, soon streamed across the Florida Straits to Camarioca and returned loaded with Cubans. The boatlift brought in some 5,000 escapees before the hurricane season ended it. But the exodus did not end. The boatlift was replaced by an airlift, an "aerial bridge."

A formal Memorandum of Understanding, signed by Cuba and the United States, established an orderly departure program, known in the United States as the Freedom Flight Program (FFP). The United States agreed to provide air transportation between Miami and Varadero "with such frequency and capacity as to permit the movement of between 3,000 and 4,000 persons per month."[20] Castro had designed a safety valve, and he was controlling it. He restricted departures; neither men of military age (fourteen through twenty-seven) nor necessary workers would be permitted to leave.

The FFP, although cheered by the Cuban communities in the United States, was not wholeheartedly supported by all Americans. Florida state and local officials feared the costs of resettling the new Cubans and the problems of relocation. Some white Floridians feared that the new influx would radically change the ethnic balance and disrupt the area politically and economically. And blacks felt threatened and angry. Those in unskilled menial and service jobs feared they would lose their jobs to the newly arriving Cubans. Blacks also resented that the federal Cuban Refugee Program afforded the newcomers greater help than state and local relief programs. Black citizens understandably resented that noncitizens received preferential treatment.[21]

The FFP, during its first year, brought more than 45,000 Cubans to Florida. Responding to the continuing influx of Cubans, Congress passed the Cuban Adjustment Act of 1966. The act allowed Cubans who entered the United States after January 1, 1959 (the beginning of Castro's regime), to adjust their status to that of permanent resident aliens, a step necessary to apply for citizenship. The Freedom Flight Program, which bridged the Johnson and Nixon administrations from 1965 to 1973, brought in more than a quarter of a million Cubans, and another 70,000 arrived from Spain. In 1973, Castro closed his safety valve and terminated the Freedom Flight Program; direct emigration from Cuba ceased. Nonetheless, by 1979 an additional 38,000 Cubans had come to the United States through third countries.[22]

"The Camarioca boatlift and the subsequent airlift," Masud-Piloto has written, "were undertaken in the absence of a clear immigration policy for refugees from Cuba. Both operations were perceived as emergencies and handled as such. Neither Johnson nor Nixon tried to normalize the immigration policy during the airlift's seven years."[23] The Castro-instigated Camarioca crisis was a foreshadowing of future Cuban refugee crises—the Mariel exodus of 1980, and the Cuban crisis of 1994. While Johnson and Nixon, and all subsequent presidents, were willing to welcome and bestow benefits on Cubans, Haitians seeking asylum received neither welcome nor aid.

No less than its policy toward Cubans, United States policy toward Haitians could be explained by the troika of interests. Foreign policy dictated that Haitian governments, no matter how vicious, be considered allies in the fight against Cuban communism. Domestic pressure groups carried little weight. The Haitian communities in the United States were economically and politically insignificant. The churches and civil rights groups that defended the Haitians were politically unimportant. The Congressional Black Caucus did not become significantly involved until the Clinton administration. And given the educational, health, and social service needs of the Haitian boat people, resettlement costs, the third interest, were perceived to be inordinately high.

Among all the groups to seek refuge in the United States, the Haitians were an anomaly. They were far fewer in number than other groups, yet they became the single-minded focus of State and Justice department efforts to bar unwanted asylum seekers. The Haitian dictatorships were among the world's most brutally repressive, yet the American government insisted that the Haitians fled for purely economic reasons. The insistence on economic motives was both deliberate and duplicitous. "Those who label groups of refugees 'economic migrants,' " observed Leo Cherne, former chairman of the International Rescue Committee, in a *New York Times* op-ed, "too often overlook the close intertwining of economic and political factors in repressive countries. . . . The expression itself— *Wirschaftsemigrant*—was coined for Hitler's victims who were seeking a haven abroad."[24]

Haiti was a country allied with us, and geopolitically critical to containing communist Cuba. Located on the western portion of the island of Hispaniola, Haiti lies across the Windward Passage, only forty miles to the southeast of Cuba. Haiti's rulers played its strategic location as a bargaining chip. The US military used Haitian ports and, during the Cuban Missile Crisis, Haitian airfields. For its part, Haiti dutifully voted in the Organization of American States to expel Cuba from the organization and impose sanctions on it. In exchange, the United States provided economic aid, while steadfastly ignoring Haiti's egregious abuse of human rights. For nearly forty years, the United States based its Haiti policy on the premise that if right-wing dictatorships were toppled, as had happened in Cuba, the resulting political disorder would invite a communist takeover.[25] From 1957 until 1994, when the United States intervened in Haiti to restore democratically elected President Jean-Bertrand Aristide, we ignored the killings, violence, terror, and repression that characterized the successive kleptocratic regimes of Papa Doc, his son Jean-Claude ("Baby Doc"), and the military oligarchies.

The Haitians themselves, however, could not ignore conditions in their country and, beginning in the late 1950s, fled to the United States, France, and other countries. Anthropologists Frederick J. Conway and Susan Huelsebusch Buchanan have described the waves of Haitian flight:

> Large-scale emigration to the United States began in the late 1950s as many middle- and upper-class Haitians, including military personnel, civil servants, and political opponents, fled the early terrors of the Duvalier period. . . . As economic and political conditions deteriorated during the 1960s, poorer, less educated Haitians joined the migrant stream. . . . Thousands of Haitians entered the United States during the late 1960s and 1970s with valid nonimmigrant visas. . . . Many of the Haitians simply overstayed their allotted time in the United States or violated the conditions of entry by accepting employment and thus joined the ranks of the undocumented. . . .
>
> The 1970s and 1980s witnessed the arrival of Haitians from the most disenfranchised and impoverished sector of Haitian society—the urban poor and the peasantry. Called boat people in the press, these Haitians preferred to risk their lives at sea rather than face intolerably bleak conditions in Haiti.[26]

The first of the Haitian boat people drifted onto the Florida shore in December of 1972. Among the sixty-five Haitians on board were twelve political prisoners who had bribed their way out of one of President-for-Life Jean-Claude Duvalier's infamous jails. They, and the family members with them, were denied the political asylum they requested; the Immigration and Naturalization Service ruled that the escaped prisoners had nothing to fear from the Haitian government.[27]

In Haiti, however, rather than the government, one feared the army, the tontons macoutes, the local section chiefs—a network of lawless thugs who owed allegiance directly to the president, who spied on the populace and subsisted on extortion. Haiti was in many ways a police state, not a tightly controlled police state with central lines of authority, such as existed in communist countries, but a state maintained by petty thieves and mercenaries. They ruled not by law, but by absolute terror, wringing tribute from the impoverished populace and enforcing their demands with arbitrary arrests, imprisonment, torture, and killings.

The early waves of Haitians, who were middle and upper class, caused no stir. But after the boat people came to the attention of the government, every administration enforced a policy that incarcerated, detained, deported, and excluded Haitians. All US administrations maintained friendly diplomatic relations with the Haitian right-wing totalitarian regimes, until the Clinton administration, in 1994, forced the departure of General Raoul Cedras.

The same troika of interests that opened the door to Cubans and closed it to Haitians also governed refugee admissions from the Soviet Union. During the Cold War and prior to the collapse of the USSR, Moscow did not allow its citizens to emigrate freely. Only three groups of Soviet citizens— ethnic Germans, Armenians, and Jews—were permitted to emigrate in significant numbers. Ethnic Germans went to the Federal Republic of Germany, Armenians emigrated to Lebanon and the United States, and Jews emigrated to Israel, other Western countries, and the United States. Moscow held refugee flows hostage to its relations with the United States.[28]

Emigration from the USSR began as a trickle in 1971 but had become a steady stream by the 1990s. (From 1982 to 1995 well over one-third of a million Soviets and former Soviets entered the United States as refugees.[29]) In the United States, Jewish pressure groups kept Russian anti-Semitism and discriminatory practices against Jews and other dissidents in the forefront of public opinion. In this, they were substantially aided by a wide spectrum of anticommunist, labor, ethnic, and religious groups. One fruit of their efforts was the passage by Congress of the Jackson-Vanik Amendment to the Trade Reform Act of 1974. The Nixon administration, in its policy of détente with the Soviets, had, in 1972, worked out a comprehensive commercial agreement with the Soviet government. As part of the agreement, the United States would extend most-favored nation (MFN) import-tariff treatment to the Soviets. But Henry Jackson in the Senate and Charles Vanik in the House of Representatives introduced an amendment to the East-West trade bill that would have blocked the extension of MFN status and credits to those countries that restricted or taxed the emigration of their citizens. Jackson-Vanik, it was thought, would pressure the Soviet Union to permit freer emigration. During the Ford administration Jackson-Vanik became part of the Trade Reform Act of 1974.[30]

The Jackson-Vanik Amendment, however, did not produce the desired effect. The Russians objected that linking MFN to emigration was an unwarranted interference in the domestic affairs of another state.[31] The trade agreement was not implemented, and the Soviets restricted emigration drastically. During the Carter administration, however, the Soviets wanted a favorable resolution of the Strategic Arms Limitation Treaty and permitted more emigration. But from the Soviet invasion of Afghanistan through the first Reagan administration, emigration continued to plummet.

The "evil empire," however, changed its emigration policy during the second Reagan administration. In early 1987, Moscow began to relax its emigration policies, and ethnic Germans, Armenians, and Jews, as well as Christian Pentecostalists, were permitted to depart. That summer, Soviet-American talks were held on emigration. And while the Soviets did not commit themselves to establishing regular emigration procedures, the number of Germans, Armenians, and Jews departing from the USSR began to rise.[32] Paradoxically, as Armenian and Jewish emigration increased, so did US budgetary problems. A senior State Department official was quoted in the *New York Times* as saying the emigration increase:

> represents a significant diplomatic achievement for the United States since higher emigration levels have long been an important goal in US-Soviet relations. However, the financial costs of accommodating refugee movement from the USSR at this level are high. . . . Without additional resources, there will be no way to avoid the suspension of all, or part, of the worldwide refugee admissions program.[33]

Along with the problem of costs came problems with a pressure group. For years ethnic groups had enthusiastically supported State Department efforts to free their countrymen. But now, for the first time, one group, the Armenians, was ambivalent. The Armenians still fervently wanted to reunite families, but they also were reluctant to have Soviet-Armenians abandon their historic homeland. The western regional director of the Armenian National Committee said: "As a policy we do not like to see Armenians leave the Soviet Union. We do not consider them political refugees."[34] The State Department acceded to the organized Armenian community; State Department lawyers now concluded that the United States was improperly accepting thousands of Armenians without the required finding that they have a well-founded fear of persecution.

As Armenian groups in the United States were withdrawing their support for massive Armenian emigration, the American embassy in Moscow, in July 1988, for budgetary reasons stopped issuing refugee visas. Financial constraints placed an absolute upper limit on the number of refugees who could be admitted. The suspension affected primarily Armenians, because the Jews seeking to emigrate to the West departed from the USSR with Israeli visas, although once in Vienna or Rome they applied for American refugee status. For the State Department's policy makers the situation was awkward. For years the United States had criticized the Soviets for erecting obstacles to emigration; now the Americans were doing it.

In Congress, thirty-two members signed a letter to President Reagan urging that visas again be issued; the Armenian Assembly of America sent a letter to Secretary of State George P. Shultz saying it was "deeply distressed" at the decision to suspend Soviet emigrant processing in "mid-course" and emphasized the hardships that would face Armenians who had applied to emigrate if they were forced to remain in the USSR. The National Conference on Soviet Jewry called the suspension "potentially tragic" and urged that the government "immediately find the funds to reinstate the activities of its Moscow embassy." And InterAction, the coordinating committee of the voluntary agencies that work with refugees, sent a letter to Secretary Shultz expressing concern about the delay in processing refugees out of the Soviet Union. The pressures had an effect. In Moscow, the processing of visas resumed.[35]

Budgetary considerations were finessed. Within the administration, the State Department's concerns over the global refugee policy were balanced against the cost-consciousness of the Office of Management and Budget. A compromise was forged; there would be higher refugee admissions numbers for fiscal year 1989, but refugee benefits in the United States would be reduced from thirty-one months to twenty-four months. Events soon overturned the budget compromise. The Soviets relaxed regulatory obstacles to emigration, and the American embassy in Moscow was deluged with applications. Slots for the first part of the budget year were quickly filled and funds depleted.[36]

As the slots filled, the rules of admission changed. No longer did those wanting to leave the Soviet Union receive virtually automatic approval. In a dramatic shift, applicants for refugee status were required to meet the "well-founded fear of persecution" standard. A significant number of Soviet Jews were now being denied refugee status. In January and February of 1989, between 15 and 16 percent of Soviet Jews had their applications denied; in March, denials soared to 37.2 percent.[37] As denials rose, the organized Jewish community went into action.

The pressure tactics produced results. Congressmen Benjamin Gilman and Hamilton Fish sent a letter to President George Bush requesting that the administration resume its policy of presuming refugee eligibility for Soviet Jews, Pentecostals, and others for the balance of the fiscal year 1989. The chairman of the House Subcommittee on Immigration, Refugees, and International Law, Bruce A. Morrison, introduced a bill to resolve the problem: Jews and Evangelical Christians, but not Armenians—in deference to Armenian pressure groups—would be considered aliens targeted for persecution. By early summer of 1989, the Bush administration had moved to allow more Soviets to emigrate, and Congress had allocated supplemental funding for refugee resettlement.[38]

But Congress did more than pass supplemental funding; it passed the Morrison-Lautenberg Amendment. The Morrison-Lautenberg Amendment requires the attorney general to establish categories of people from the Soviet Union, Vietnam, Laos, and Cambodia "who share common characteristics that would identify them as targets of persecution." Under the amendment, a member of a category group can establish a well-founded fear of persecution "by asserting such fear and asserting a credible basis for concern about the possibility of such persecution."[39] The Morrison-Lautenberg Amendment applied a more relaxed standard for these countries and reopened the door for Soviet refugees.

During the Bush administration, emigration from the Soviet Union rose dramatically; well over 200,000 persons entered the United States between 1988 and 1992.[40] In response to the steady emigration, since 1990 the Jackson-Vanik Amendment has been waived, first by President Bush and then by President Clinton. In 1994, Clinton, after first securing the endorsement of major American Jewish groups, including the National Conference on Soviet Jewry, the leading monitor of Soviet Jewish emigration, made automatic the granting of the annual waiver. Henceforth, Russia will maintain its favored trade status. Nonetheless, since only Congress can repeal Jackson-Vanik, it remains as law. Russia continues to be subject to the terms of the law, including a requirement that the State Department report twice a year to Congress about Russia's emigration practices. Should Russia revert to its past policy of capping emigration, the automatic waiver could be repealed.[41]

Under the Clinton administration, emigration from Russia and other countries of the former Soviet Union continued at high levels. But the conditions of the communist era that justified a refugee program have changed. Communism no longer holds sway in Eastern Europe. The Union of Soviet Socialist Republics has disintegrated and with it the strict impediments to departure. The high levels of emigration, in-country processing in Russia, and the lowered threshold of proof of persecution mandated by the Morrison-Lautenberg Amendment have turned what was once a refugee program into a specialized immigration stream. Nonetheless, on April 30, 1994, President Clinton signed into law an extension of the Lautenberg Amendment until September 30, 1996. Armenians in Azerbaijan, since the fighting between Azerbaijan and Armenia, are threatened by violence directed against them. Armenian pressure groups, concerned about the safety of their ethnic kin, have petitioned Attorney General Janet Reno to include Armenians from Azerbaijan as a designated category under the Lautenberg Amendment.[42]

Along with the Soviet Union, the Lautenberg Amendment covers refugees from Vietnam, Laos, and Cambodia. Like the refugee streams from the Soviet Union, the Southeast Asian refugee streams were manipulated by power politics. The strongest interest of the troika, foreign policy, governed their admission into the United States.

President Richard M. Nixon, who resigned from the presidency in disgrace in 1974, bequeathed the denouement of the Vietnam War to his successor, Gerald Ford. In the spring of 1975, the South Vietnamese government disintegrated, and the United States began evacuating Americans and Vietnamese from Saigon. That May, while the evacuees were being brought into the United States, a Harris poll revealed that only 36 percent of all Americans thought Indochinese should be admitted, and 54 percent thought they should be excluded. California Congressman Burt Talcott succinctly summed up the racist view when he urged the government not to bring in refugees because, in his words, "Damn it, we have too many Orientals."[43] Governors, senators, and congressmen, in a fervor of nativism, urged Washington to proceed with caution in bringing in the Indochinese.[44]

Congress, despite the restrictionist fervor, responded to the exodus with the passage of the Indochina Migration and Refugee Act of 1975. The act provided statutory authorization for a temporary program of relief and resettlement. Some 135,00 refugees were evacuated, screened on Guam and Wake Island, and processed through reception centers in the United States. By the end of year, the temporary refugee relocation camps had been closed. But the agony of Indochina was not over. Refugees continued to leave Vietnam, Laos, and Cambodia. The Migration Act was subsequently extended and ultimately replaced by the 1980 Refugee Act.

In Vietnam, the "new order" impelled the departure of waves of "gold bar" refugees and "boat people." In Laos, shortly after the fall of Saigon, the communist Pathet Lao took control of the government, and America's wartime allies, the Hmong, were forced to flee. In Cambodia, following the turmoil and bloodshed of the Khmer Rouge genocide and Vietnam's invasion, the numbers of refugees swelled. "Feet people" and "boat people" poured into the neighboring countries of Thailand, Malaysia, and Singapore, creating unprecedented economic and political problems. President Carter, in July 1978, ordered American ships to pick up the boat people, promising them resettlement in the United States. Carter's order was intended to spur an international response to the exodus.

The United Nations High Commissioner for Refugees called a special meeting of nations in Geneva, Switzerland, in December 1978, but the convocation produced meager results. More success was found some months later, at the First International Conference on Indochinese Refugees. The UNHCR and the Socialist Republic of Vietnam concluded a Memorandum of Understanding and established an Orderly Departure Program (ODP). Under the ODP, the Vietnamese government authorized the exit of people who wished to leave Vietnam and settle in foreign countries. But exit permits were issued at the will of the Vietnamese government and were far fewer than wanted. As a result, clandestine land and boat departures continued.[45]

Refugee admissions from Southeast Asia, originally conceived as a short-term program, have continued for more than two decades. Despite the high costs and difficulties of resettling the Southeast Asians, and the sometimes strong sentiment against them, the views of the Department of State (DOS) prevailed. The DOS pursued a foreign policy that was staunchly anticommunist and at the same time wanted to stabilize the noncommunist countries in the region. (Migrants threatened the economic and political stability of neighboring countries.) These pragmatic reasons were reinforced by feelings of guilt over having abandoned our allies and a humanitarian concern for the plight of the escapees.

The broad-based Citizens' Commission on Indochinese Refugees, formed by Leo Cherne, the chairman of the International Rescue Committee, aided the State Department in its admissionist stance. Gil Loescher and John A. Scanlan have described its effectiveness:

> The Citizens' Commission secured support from numerous national organizations, including labor unions, ethnic associations, religious groups, and a wide range of other organizations. Supporters ran the gamut from the National Council of Jewish Women, the American Council of Voluntary Agencies for Foreign Service, the US Catholic Conference, the American Jewish Committee, Freedom House, the Anti-Defamation League of B'nai Brith, and Social Democrats USA to the Coalition for a Democratic Majority. Undoubtedly, many blacks feared the effects of a massive influx of refugees. Yet by enlisting the endorsements of over eighty prominent black leaders, including all the black mayors in the country, who called on the Carter administration to accept Indochinese refugees "in the same spirit that we have urged our country to accept the victims of South Africa's apartheid," the Citizens' Commission neutralized potential opposition. AFL-CIO Chairman George Meany hand-delivered both to Carter and [Secretary of State Cyrus] Vance his own personal appeal urging that administration policy be based on the findings and recommendations of the Commission.[46]

Foreign policy objectives and artful lobbying have enabled Southeast Asians to enter the United States under a variety of programs. Some have come as refugees after having reached a neighboring country where they were held in detention camps. Some have been rescued at sea. Others have come directly from Vietnam under the Orderly Departure Program and have been admitted, depending on their eligibility status, as refugees, parolees, or immigrants. Amerasians—persons fathered by Americans before the United States withdrew in 1975—and their family members are admitted under the Amerasian Homecoming Act (AHA) of 1988 as immigrants but are entitled to refugee assistance benefits and social services. The AHA has no "sunset" provision, and small numbers of Amerasians and their accompanying relatives will continue to arrive in the United States for the foreseeable future.[47]

Since 1975 approximately 1,200,000 Southeast Asian refugees have fled their homelands and entered the United States. Of the arrivals the largest number is of Vietnamese (more than 700,000), followed by Laotians (some 250,000) and Cambodians (some 150,000). Amerasian program entrants have been the smallest number (more than 70,000).[48]

Southeast Asian refugees no longer command the daily headlines. Their entrance into the United States has shrunk from a floodtide to a steady, but diminishing, trickle. Washington has moved to normalize relations with Hanoi and Phnom Penh. In the summer of 1995, Cambodia reopened its embassy in Washington, and the Clinton administration has extended full diplomatic recognition to Vietnam.[49]

The agony of the Vietnam War is over. In Europe communism is dead. Germany has been reunited. The Baltic states and the Soviet satellite states in Eastern Europe are free. The Cold War against the Union of Soviet Socialist Republics has been won. The former constituent republics of the USSR are struggling with the problems of newfound independence. American foreign policy, no longer fighting Soviet-style communism, is instead seeking to shore up former communist societies now embracing nascent capitalist economies.

The United States' refugee policy, however, is still locked in a Cold War mentality. The Clinton administration in August 1995 proposed 90,000 refugee slots for fiscal year 1996. Of this number, seven-ninths are from the former Soviet Union and Eastern Europe (45,000) and from Southeast Asia (25,000). Migrants from East Asia and the former Soviet Union, it should be remembered, are permitted entrance to the United States under the Lautenberg Amendment's lower standard of refugee eligibility. The remaining places, two-ninths, are reserved for Africa (7,000), Latin America and the Caribbean (6,000), the Near East and South Asia (4,000), and an unallocated reserve (3,000).[50] (The Latin America and Caribbean numbers are supplemented by the September 1994 United States–Cuban Migration Accord which committed the United States to admit at least 20,000 Cubans annually.)

Only a meager 17,000 slots are allocated for persons who meet the universal standard of persecution set forth by the UN convention and the 1967 protocol. This standard was incorporated into the Refugee Act of 1980 and was intended to be the standard for United States refugee admissions. When the Refugee Act was being drafted, the House Judiciary Committee report emphasized that "the plight of the refugees themselves as opposed to national-origin or political considerations should be paramount in determining which refugees are to be admitted to the United States."[51] The ideological and geographical biases included in all previous refugee legislation were to be jettisoned, the domestic definition was to be linked to the international definition, and the humanitarian and nondiscriminatory aspects of the law were to be emphasized. This has not happened in either refugee or asylee admissions.

Since the passage of the Refugee Act, the prime beneficiaries of the controlling troika of interests have been Southeast Asians, Cubans, émigrés from Eastern Europe, the USSR, and now the former Soviet Union and its republics. In the years since its passage, the major provisions of the Refugee Act, ideologically neutral admissions and a fair asylum policy, have never been implemented.

The UN convention and the 1967 protocol clearly state that refuges be outside their country of origin, yet the vast majority of refugees received by the United States have come not from refugee camps or countries of first asylum, but directly to the United States through the mechanism of "in-country processing." In-country processing is now the modus operandi for most of the US refugee programs, applying to Lautenberg Amendment Vietnamese and Soviets. What were originally refugee flows have now become "managed migration."[52]

Managed migration, for the host country, offers the benefit of control. The host country can screen applicants and place a cap on the numbers admitted; arrivals of refugees can be scheduled and their resettlement planned. Managed migration, by its very nature, is the antithesis of mass escape—sudden, unanticipated arrivals of large numbers of asylum seekers. The Refugee Act addresses refugees and asylum seekers; for a vast majority of those admitted through its refugee program, the United States has adopted orderly procedures for admission, procedures which for Soviets, Vietnamese, and Cubans seem more appropriate to an immigration than a mass escape program. But the Refugee Act never addressed the problem of mass escape. Significantly, the first challenge to the Refugee Act would be a crisis of mass escape—the Mariel boatlift.

3
The Mariel Floodtide: Mass Escape

Key West, Florida, in mid-April of 1980, was in clamorous chaos, like a latter-day gold rush town. Cuban-Americans swarmed the docks with fists, pockets, briefcases, suitcases crammed with cash. Boat owners leaped to the opportunity, chartering or even selling their boats to the highest bidders. Store owners, too, profited as their shelves were briskly emptied of everything from food to fuel. In Cuba, Castro had just opened the port of Mariel, and Americans reacted with a kind of frontier riotousness. The sea lanes were choked with boats heading to Cuba. From Washington had come threats that boats returning from Cuba would be subjected to fines or seizure, but Cuban exiles and boat owners alike freely ignored the warnings. The Coast Guard, which should have seized the illegal boats, had all it could do to rescue disabled boats too small to make the trip.

Three weeks later, the townspeople of Key West were voicing their condemnation. Business had fallen off; hotels, restaurants, boutiques, and scuba shops were feeling the pinch. The Chamber of Commerce was getting seventy-five to a hundred phone calls a day from anxious vacationers asking, "Is it safe to walk on the streets? Are the Cubans visible? Is there food in the restaurants? Is there gas in the gas stations, or are the Cubans using it all in their boats?" Most of all, the tourists feared that rapists and robbers were roaming the streets.[1] Secret nightmares had found their reality. Refugees were draining America's wealth, consuming our resources. They threatened our well-being; they were violent and uncontrolled.

By December, order had been restored, and Key West was again a small community struggling to meet its budget. "As for the Cubans," Mayor Charles McCoy announced, "the reports that they were raping, terrorizing and spreading disease in Key West were totally fabricated. Most of them didn't even see Key West because after landing in the restricted area they were immediately flown out or driven out of the city. But these irresponsible stories practically ruined our 1980 tourist season."[2]

Key West is the southernmost point in the United States, and it was the first point of entry for the Mariel entrants. From there, we can look north and west and see what was to happen in the entire country, not just during the Mariel boatlift, but also in the years since. Before Mariel, Washington used refugee flow as a weapon in its foreign policy arsenal; now Cuba had wrested that weapon from Washington and turned it against the United States. Outside Washington, an American public at first welcomed the arriving heroes but quickly came to resent and to fear them. The resentment and fear have persisted, although they have little foundation in reality. But the mass escape movement that was the Mariel boatlift altered the course of American history.

Mass escape movements do not spring suddenly into existence and as suddenly disappear. Mass escape movements have deep roots and long branches. The Mariel boatlift of 1980 did not begin in April of that year, and it did not end in October. Its roots were formed more than twenty years before, and its branches continue to grow today. The roots of the Mariel boatlift lay first in Cuba and Haiti—in the political and economic conditions in those two countries and in our responses to them. Mariel also had its roots in this country—in the way previous migrations of Cubans and Haitians had been received and integrated. Mariel's branches, as well, were both foreign and domestic. Unresolved issues from the boatlift continue to influence United States policy even now. The ashes of Mariel banked the fires of restrictionism that grow stronger each year. That restrictionism fed the decision, in 1994, to reverse decades of American policy toward Cuba and Haiti. And that restrictionism still influences voter attitudes and domestic policies.

The earliest roots were formed nearly forty years ago. Cubans first fled when Batista was ousted and the flow of Cuban escapees has lasted longer than any other; they continue to leave today under a United States and Cuban immigration/escape program. American foreign policy dictated that we would give all Cubans arriving in this country refugee status, resettle and assist them. The Cuban Adjustment Act, in effect since 1966, allows any Cuban arriving in the United States—whether a tourist who overstayed a visa or an undocumented boat person—to acquire permanent residency, the first step toward citizenship. Cubans were welcomed as political refugees, often assisted in leaving Cuba, sometimes rescued at sea and brought to the United States. An anticommunist foreign policy welcomed Cubans, and as more Cubans arrived and joined an already well-established community, the Cuban-Americans became an influential pressure group.

Anticommunism and an influential pressure group, the two key elements of the refugee troika, were absent for the Haitians. Foreign policy worked against them. The State Department relied on the Duvaliers, father and son, and later the military oligarchy to help contain Castro's communism. And there never developed a wealthy and politically powerful Haitian community to lobby for admission. So Haitians, in contrast to Cubans, were rejected as economic refugees, discouraged from departure, rejected for asylum, and held in detention. By December of 1979, over 600,000 Cubans had come directly to the United States. Nine thousand Haitians had also requested political asylum, but only fifty-five had received it. The contrast in reception was described by Edward A. McCarthy, the Catholic archbishop of Miami. In a 1979 letter to President Carter, the archbishop observed:

> Only recently, while the United States Department of Immigration office in Miami was deeply involved with attempting to exclude or deport Haitians, a Cuban who arrived in a small raft was speedily processed and given indefinite voluntary departure status which in two years would make him eligible for permanent United States residence and, in five years from date of arrival, for United States citizenship. Haitians who arrive at the same time and under similar circumstances are incarcerated and in five years may still be pleading their cases in court, if they have not already been deported.[3]

More roots were formed as local communities resented having to bear the burden for those refugees, such as the Haitians, whom the federal government neither resettled nor assisted. Dewey W. Knight, Jr., assistant Dade County, Florida, manager, urged that the Haitians be given the opportunity to work and to receive community services, opportunities that their lack of legal status denied them. Most important, he asked for "Federal resources to assist people who are clearly a Federal charge." The cost in 1979 to Dade County, which includes Miami, for providing services to Haitians was $2,747,000. (That figure was considerably less than that expended on "legal" entrants, such as the Cubans. By 1980, when the Refugee Act phased out the Cuban Program, federal expenditures to resettle Cubans had reached $1.4 billion.[4]) Dade County was beginning to be resentful that the federal government failed to reimburse the local communities for Haitians as it did for Cubans. South Florida—and later other areas in the country— would be willing to bear the responsibility for refugees but insisted that it not be required to bear the costs.

The arrival of the Cubans, moreover, had engendered resentment not only because they had been favored over other asylum seekers. It also appeared to many that the Cubans had been favored over American citizens. The black community in South Florida was angry at having lost jobs to the Cuban arrivals. Writing to President Lyndon Johnson, Donald Wheeler Jones, president of the Miami Beach Branch of the NAACP, observed that Cubans had replaced blacks as "waiters, bell-hops, doormen, elevator operators, and other . . . menial, service type jobs that require a minimum of formal education or training."[5] Moreover, in Florida's school system,

Cuban children went to "white" schools, while black children remained segregated. And again, the Cubans, as refugees, were eligible for greater amounts and more kinds of assistance than were made available to members of the black community.

Despite the resentment, however, one of the most striking aspects of the Mariel boatlift would be the preference shown by the government to the Cuban arrivals over the Haitians. This preference persisted even though the number of arriving Haitians was, and always had been, a fraction of the number of Cubans we received. The Cubans, unlike the Haitians, had a powerful community to pressure politically for their admission and to assist in their resettlement. Cuban-Americans were well placed to find jobs and housing for the new-comers; Haitians in this country could not provide the same support. And even though each succeeding wave of Cuban arrivals came with less wealth and lower levels of education and skills than the previous one, even in the Mariel boatlift the arriving Cubans were healthier and better educated than the arriving Haitians. But the strongest basis for this preference was the United States' rigid anticommunism.

The Mariel crisis also had more immediate roots in American relations with Cuba, relations that, despite our rigid anticommunism, were inconsistent. The United States and Cuba had recently clashed on the question of Cuban political prisoners. In 1978, Fidel Castro had agreed to release three thousand political prisoners, and another six hundred prisoners who had tried to leave the island illegally, on condition that they be admitted to the United States. The United States had long demanded that Castro release his political prisoners, yet Attorney General Griffin Bell, fearing the infiltration of "communists, terrorists, and criminals," insisted on personally screening each prisoner. Although four hundred prisoners were to have been admitted each month, after two months, Bell had approved the admission of only forty-six.[6] Eighteen months later, in early April of 1980, one thousand released political prisoners and their families remained in Cuba.[7]

Not only political prisoners, but any Cuban wishing to emigrate fell victim to an inconsistent US policy. Wayne S. Smith, who was chief of the US Interests Section in Havana from 1979 to 1982, observed that the Cubans "complained that while we welcomed anyone who arrived in Florida by small boat, we offered very few immigrant visas. . . ."[8]

Between 1973 and 1979, only 38,000 Cubans arrived in the United States, most of them through third countries.[9] Clearly, there was greater propaganda value in small groups of sunburned, half-starved refugees escaping in flimsy boats than there was in immigrants regularly arriving by plane. Possibly for that reason, while the United States prosecuted Cuban plane hijackers, we did not prosecute boat hijackers.

It was precisely that failure of the United States to prosecute boat hijackers that most rankled Castro and perhaps led directly to his opening the Mariel harbor. When Carter became president, the United States entered into discussions with Cuba, discussions intended to establish more cooperative relations between the two countries. A major thorn in those relations, for Castro, had been the boat hijackings from Cuba. When the United States did not address the issue, the thorn festered. Wayne Smith was told that "if we insisted on encouraging the arrival of people in small boats . . . Cuba could give us more than we could handle."[10] On March 8, Castro himself renewed the threat, saying:

> We hope they will adopt measures so they will not encourage the illegal departures from the country because we might also have to take our own measures. We did it once. . . . We were forced to take measures in this regard once. We have also warned them of this. We once had to open the Camarioca port. . . . We feel it is proof of the lack of maturity of the US Government to again create similar situations.[11]

The State Department ignored the warning.

In Cuba, animosity was growing toward the United States. The CIA, as early as January, had warned of a possible "large-scale emigration to reduce discontent caused by Cuba's deteriorating economic condition." The CIA described a stagnating Cuban economy, in which "a rapidly expanding labor force has created a labor surplus, and many recently graduated Cuban youths have been unable to obtain jobs."[12] Cuba's straitened economy seemed all the more austere when Cuban-American exiles visited the island, bringing sorely needed American currency and flaunting their American "wealth."

For its part, the State Department, which had publicly portrayed Castro as a great danger to the security of the United States, privately failed to address his threats seriously. The Refugee Act was shortly to take effect, and the State Department believed that, under the act, an allocation of one thousand refugees a month from Cuba for fiscal year 1980 would satisfy the Castro government and relieve domestic pressure in Cuba.[13] Although the State Department consistently labeled the Cuban arrivals "political refugees"—as opposed to the Haitian "economic migrants"—the pressure that Castro was feeling was economic, not political. If the United States were to admit one thousand political dissidents each month, that would hardly have relieved Cuba's economic pressures. On the other hand, admitting the economically dissatisfied would have been a cynical misreading of the Refugee Act and a distortion of the concept of refugee admissions.

On April 20, 1980, Fidel Castro opened the port of Mariel in Cuba and announced that Cubans were free to leave by boat. From that date, the Mariel crisis was inevitable, not because of Castro's decision but because of decisions made over the previous fifteen years, decisions that had built an avalanche of inevitability.

The first rock in that avalanche had been the Camarioca boatlift. Fifteen years earlier, Camarioca had demonstrated to Castro that he had a powerful weapon to use against the United States. When, in April of 1973, the regular airlifts that had superseded the Camarioca boatlift halted, 150,000 Cubans, with entry documents to join their families in the United States, were left stranded. Those Cubans, and others, were further inflamed when the exile visits were resumed; more than 100,000 Cuban-Americans visited their families in Cuba bringing tales of a better life and embellishing those tales with over $100 million in spending.[14]

Other promises had been conveyed as well. Both in this country and in Cuba, it was expected that all Cubans arriving on our shores would be welcomed, given permanent residency and resettlement assistance. Whatever their individual reasons for emigrating might have been, Cubans arriving in this country were heralded as freedom fighters, were proclaimed to have "voted with their feet" for democracy and freedom. The Cuban-American community regarded refugee status for their compatriots as an entitlement, a view that was shared by many in the government. But one important promise had been broken—the promise to speedily process and resettle the released political prisoners. It is ironic that the single group of people who were unquestionably entitled to immediate political asylum were those being kept in a state of indetermination.

The Mariel boatlift began, as it would end six months later, with an order from Castro. Through the winter and early spring of 1980, Cubans had been forcing their way into Latin American embassies and demanding asylum. On April 1, a bus carrying six Cubans crashed through the fence surrounding the Peruvian embassy, killing a guard. Castro reinforced the guards and barricades at the embassy. Suddenly, three days later, Castro reversed himself and reopened the embassy grounds. Cuban radio made an announcement that anyone wishing to leave the country could go to the Peruvian embassy; Cubans by the thousands rushed to the compound. On Easter Sunday, April 6, Castro again closed the embassy grounds, sealing the Cubans inside. The would-be émigrés had, by now, become a *cause célèbre* in the Cuban exile communities. Demonstrations were held in New York and Miami and money, food, and relief supplies were donated.

By April 10, it had been arranged that the embassy Cubans would be flown to Costa Rica, there to await resettlement in third countries. Four days later, the United States announced that it would accept 3,500 of the escapees through an orderly departure program. The Cubans would be screened and processed in San Jose, then flown to the United States. President Carter allocated $4.25 million for the transportation and resettlement of the Cubans.

Although it was only a precursor to the actual Mariel boatlift, the American response to the events at the Peruvian embassy was in a sense a fruition and a microcosm of the past twenty years. Instantly, the embassy Cubans were romanticized, given the sobriquet of the Havana Ten Thousand (although their actual numbers were closer to seven thousand). Newspapers across the country gave vent to bursts of hyperbole. The *New York Times* editorialized:

> That kind of determination warrants a generous American response. A fleet of the largest available ships ought to be sent in to extricate the Havana Ten Thousand. And they should be welcomed in the United States if they wish to settle here.[15]

The *Chicago Tribune* published an encomium to the Cubans, pronouncing that people "whose spirit cannot be contained in the stultifying sameness of totalitarianism are the ones who chose to leave it."[16] In fact, the Cubans who crowded into the embassy compound had a range of reasons for leaving; for some those reasons were intertwined with earlier American policies and practices. There were many former political prisoners and their families in the compound. One woman told a reporter that her husband had twice been a political prisoner, the second time serving a sentence of ten years. The husband had applied for the American parole program for himself, his wife, and their three children. But the United States was accepting only prisoners released *after* August 1, 1978 (when the agreement had been reached with Castro), and the man had been rejected. The family thought to take their chances at the embassy, but they were arrested and the husband taken prisoner again.[17]

Many more were driven by economic deprivation. Tobacco and sugar crops had fallen victim to natural disasters, drought and insects. The economy as a whole had fallen victim to world inflation and an embargo by the United States. Still other Cubans were being driven out, by the government or by community pressure. Homosexuals were regarded in Cuba as criminals; the unemployed were called antisocial.

Not only the press and the public, but the government itself responded confusedly to the Cuban escapees. When Carter announced that the United States would accept 3,500 Cubans from Costa Rica, that number was to be one-third of the purported 10,000. No reasons were given for how that quota was determined. It is possible that one-third was regarded as a "fair share" of the total, leaving two-thirds to be resettled by other countries in the region. But one-third would not have been a fair share, given the relative size and wealth of the United States. More important, the United States embargo had contributed to Cuba's economic decline, America's previous history of welcome and the exile visits of Cuban-Americans had encouraged many Cubans to see the United States as their promised land, and the ill-managed parole of political prisoners left thousands stranded.

All the Cubans in the Peruvian embassy compound—political refugees and would-be immigrants together—were to be evacuated and resettled somewhere. Once more, a clear message had been sent that any Cuban who could leave his country would be resettled elsewhere, very possibly in the United States. This message, which had been delivered so many times over the previous two decades, would quickly come to haunt us.

On April 18, when only 1,500 of the Cubans in the Peruvian embassy compound had been flown to San Jose, Castro suddenly cut off the flights. The next day, thirty boats left the United States, carrying food and medical supplies for the embassy Cubans. When those boats reached the port of Mariel on April 20, the Cuban government announced abruptly that the port was open; the American captains were free to take their friends and relatives.

On April 21, three groups of actors, one in Florida, one in Washington, and one in Havana, tried out their new roles. In Florida, some sixty Cuban exile boat captains met in Key West, at the auspiciously named Fourth of July restaurant, and planned to leave for Cuba. Almost immediately hundreds of boats were chartered for the voyage. The Cuban-American community had moved beyond lobbying and was now in charge of the troika of interests.

In Washington, the administration proffered an ineffectual gesture of control, warning that returning boats would be fined $1,000 for each passenger they brought back. The threat of fines was meaningless. The Cuban exile community had, for twenty years, been animated by two desires—the reunification of their families and the overthrow of Castro. With this new boatlift, the first desire could become a reality and the second would be closer to achievement. The fines would be no more than a small tax on the price of each family member's passage.

In Havana, Castro began giving exit permits to Cubans who had not been at the Peruvian embassy. Boat captains arriving in Mariel presented officials with a list of friends and relatives, whom the officials would then locate and bring by bus to the port. Cuban-Americans were phoning relatives in Cuba, telling them to prepare to leave by boat. Cubans were calling their relatives in this country, asking them to send boats to pick them up. Phone lines were quickly swamped, and Cuba reserved hundreds of long-distance lines for priority calls to the United States.[18] (By early May, the Cuban government was applying a formula to the departures: 30 percent of the passengers on a returning boat could be family members and friends, the remainder were selected from embassy demonstrators and from people whom Castro wanted to deport.)

By May 1, over five thousand Cubans had landed in Florida in a stream of boats that had by now been dubbed the Freedom Flotilla. The United States government, unable to control the crisis, had seized only three boats.

The setting was in place, the various members of the cast were playing their parts, and the American public was watching intently. But the drama was becoming absurd. The two leading actors, Fidel Castro in Havana and Jimmy Carter in Washington, acted erratically and unpredictably. Some of the supporting American cast, the Congress and the various government and enforcement agencies, performed seemingly without direction, without even, perhaps, a script. Other players, the Cuban exile and the black and anglo communities, performed without regard to the other actors on the stage. And finally, the audience, the American public was becoming restless and loud, some of them demanding that the curtain be brought down.

The leading actor in the drama would be Fidel Castro. Castro had repeatedly expressed anger that the United States encouraged Cuban boat hijackers. The United States had been like the sorcerer, calling for buckets of water. And Castro had suddenly become the sorcerer's apprentice, drowning the master in his own demands. A few boats from Cuba gave the United States a propaganda tool, a torrent of them gave Castro a powerful weapon.

Castro was also using the Mariel boatlift to remove another, still larger thorn from his flesh. He had agreed to the release of the political prisoners because they were an impediment to his revolution, an acknowledgment that there were Cuban citizens who would not march to his drummer. There were other prisoners as well, individuals who had never assimilated into the new Cuban society. Castro had chafed at the United States not removing his political prisoners quickly enough. Now he had an opportunity to rid himself of all the "social misfits," Castro had warned that he might do so.

Responding to Castro's actions was Jimmy Carter. Another president might have transformed the Mariel crisis into a triumph; under Carter it became a disaster.[19] The year 1980 was an election year, Florida an important state where Carter was being attacked by Republican primary candidates Ronald Reagan and George Bush. Cubans had settled in concentrated areas, primarily in Miami and surrounding Dade County, but also in the New York–New Jersey metropolitan area. This geographic concentration, coupled with Cuban economic strength, made Cubans a powerful pressure group. In Florida, there were two important constituencies—the Cuban exile community and the non-Hispanic white community, called "anglo." By the time the boatlift ended, Carter had alienated both.

Carter faced other problems at the same time. Mariel involved foreign policy, and Carter was preoccupied with the American hostages in Iran and the Soviet invasion of Afghanistan.[20] Mariel incurred social and economic costs, and the country was in a recession, with loss of jobs and cutbacks in government spending. But Carter, whom many considered to be a weak president, intensified that perception when he not only failed to enunciate a clear policy but several times within the first several weeks shifted his policy positions.

On April 25, the administration announced its intention to halt the boatlift. Although that position was politically controversial, it was necessary because the country was in a recession. New immigrants would compete for jobs and housing at a time when both were scarce; they would require social services, and local communities would need federal reimbursement, yet the government was cutting back its spending.[21]

Funding would prove contentious in another way as well. Although the new Refugee Act no longer gave preference to refugees from communist countries, early in the boatlift arriving Cubans were given applications for political asylum, cash, and medical assistance; Haitians were given no such assistance.[22] Moreover, although government officials had resolved not to perpetuate previous injustices against the Haitians, President Carter continued to exacerbate the problem. On May 7, he issued a formal declaration that the Federal Emergency Management Agency (FEMA) would coordinate all agencies involved in the emergency. But the declaration failed to include the Haitians, so that FEMA officials refused to authorize funding, programs, or services for the Haitians.[23]

Suddenly, on May 5, Carter made an astonishing announcement. After a speech to the League of Women Voters convention in Washington, he responded to a question about enforcing United States immigration laws by promising, "We'll continue to provide an open heart and open arms to refugees seeking freedom from Communist domination and from the economic deprivation brought about primarily by Fidel Castro and his government." In effect, Carter had just asserted that the United States would not turn back *any* Cuban escapee. Swept along by his rhetoric, he went on to pledge that Cubans and Haitians would receive "the same degree of compassion and understanding."[24] Since he had just announced open arms for Cubans, this new policy implied, by extension, that Haitians, too, would now have to be resettled.

An open-door policy clearly was a bid for disaster, and Carter shortly had to reverse himself again. On May 14, he presented a new plan for the admission of Cuban escapees. He would

> permit safe and orderly passage from Cuba, for those people who sought freedom in the US Interest Section in Havana first of all; for political prisoners who have been held by Castro for many years; for those who sought a haven of freedom in the Peruvian Embassy, some of whom [were] still being held there; and for close family members of Cuban-Americans who live in this country and who have permanent resident status. Those four categories will be given priority in their authorization to come to our country.

Carter went on, "We are ready to start an airlift and a sealift for these screened and qualified people to come to our country and for *no other escapees* from Cuba."[25] (Italics added.)

What President Carter was proposing was an orderly departure program (ODP). Such a program had been in place for one year for refugees from Vietnam. Under an orderly departure program, refugees can be screened and processed for resettlement before they leave their countries. When such a program is in place, its advantages are many. First, as the title indicates, departures from the country of origin are orderly; refugees do not risk their lives in unsafe escapes. Second, the refugees are assured of resettlement before they leave; they do not remain indefinitely in refugee camps. For the receiving country, there are also clear advantages. The numbers of refugees are controlled. It is possible to plan in advance for funding and for resettlement. But ODP, while a desirable option, is not always possible. The first requirement of an ODP program is the cooperation of the sending government. That government must permit the screening to be carried out and must allow for the protection of refugees while they are awaiting evacuation.

But Castro's assistance in an orderly departure program had not been engaged, since no negotiations were taking place. We had pronounced the policy, but we could not put it into practice. Cubans continued to arrive from Cuba, not in orderly air- and sealifts, after screening and processing, but in the same uncontrolled and unregulated flow as previously.

On May 20, Jack Watson, a presidential assistant in charge of the Mariel crisis, announced that Cubans arriving in Florida would be considered not refugees but applicants for asylum.[26] Under the Refugee Act, refugees were subject to annual ceilings, arrived at after consultation between the White House and Congress. No such ceilings obtained for asylees. Moreover, the law entitled refugees, but not asylum seekers, to federally financed assistance. Far from solving problems, Carter had only complicated them beyond understanding.

By that date, May 20, some 62,000 Cubans had arrived by boat; countless more were coming. Perhaps 10,000 Haitians had also arrived. Unlike refugee determinations, asylum decisions are made individually; each asylum seeker's case must be individually reviewed and individually determined. The sheer number of claims would take years to review. And during that time, South Florida would have to provide jobs, housing, social services, and education for tens of thousands but would not be eligible for the federal assistance mandated by the Refugee Act. This latest "policy" did not solve any problems but only deferred them. Eventually, a determination of status would have to be made for the Cubans and the Haitians not as individuals, but as a group. Eventually, federal assistance would have to be given to the states and local communities. The White House could only have hoped to take these actions later, rather than sooner. The White House was negotiating a path between two opposing interests: on one side, the Cuban exile community; on the other, the black and the anglo communities. Each side represented votes.

The black community sorely resented the latest influx of Cubans. Earlier waves of Cubans had taken the unskilled jobs and low-rent housing that had belonged to the blacks. As the economy weakened, no new jobs or housing had replaced them. A new wave of Cubans would only exacerbate the competition. The non-Hispanic white community also resented the Cubans. They saw a cultural shift in South Florida and were threatened by it. Some Miami residents protested the arrivals with signs that read "Save America for Us" and "Learn and Speak English, Dammit."[27] While many—black, white, and Hispanic—welcomed and assisted the escapees, the state of Florida and the local communities chafed under the financial burden they felt should have been borne by the federal government.

On one side Cuban exiles were demanding that Carter admit *all* the escapees and that he not negotiate with Castro. On another side, the blacks and non-Hispanic whites were demanding that Carter shut down the boatlift, even if that meant he had to negotiate with Castro. And in the middle was the state of Florida, asserting that while many of the Cubans would make valuable citizens (a nod to the Cubans), most should be resettled outside South Florida (a nod to the blacks and anglos). Alongside Florida were the other states to which the Cubans were now being sent, which further demanded (in a nod to the taxpayers) that the federal government reimburse the receiving communities.

Carter negotiated his way through this thicket of competing interests as though he was following a trail of bread crumbs. Some of the crumbs were eaten by birds, the rest were scattered by the wind, and he was left with no visible trail. He wound up circling in place, haunted by a single fear—that barring Cubans from our shores could, in the words of Victor Palmieri, the refugee coordinator, "push [the Cuban exile community] into widespread civil disorder and even armed insurrection."[28] Administration sources told reporters for the *Miami Herald* that this single fear, the fear of "bombings and riots in Miami," not only overrode all other considerations but led Carter to pursue a deception. Publicly, the administration threatened to shut down the boatlift; privately, the administration resolved to permit it.[29] Early on, the White House had announced that it would interdict and prosecute boat owners leaving for Mariel. The policy was never put into effect. Ronald Copeland, who served on the refugee coordinator's staff during Mariel, believes that "uncertainty at the policy level created confusion at the operations level."[30]

It remains unclear just why Carter was swayed by threats from the Cuban community. Equally powerful were threats from the black community. Palmieri himself warned that they were "heading for a long, hot summer, and if the numbers get really high, there could be a reaction reminiscent of what happened in the city ghettos in the 1960s."[31] And there was an equally strong possibility of white backlash. An aide to Florida Representative Claude Pepper observed that "for the first time, the hate mail that was coming in was signed."[32] It was not one segment of the South Florida voters that needed to be placated, but an entire region that threatened to explode.

An editorial in the *Miami Herald* argued that Carter must not cave in to the threat of violence but must resist it. The newspaper staff had met with Victor Palmieri, who conceded:

> The President decided not to try to prevent the illegal sealift, nor to stop it early on, because local law-enforcement officials unanimously advised against action. The lawmen, he said, feared violence by Cuban-Americans if the Administration tried to prevent them from illegally going to Mariel, Cuba, to bring out their relatives.

The editorial continued:

> Think about that for a moment. The President consciously let the threat of mob reaction intimidate him into ignoring the law and allowing his own policies to be trampled. When the President finally ordered the boatlift halted on May 15, he did so because the Cuban-American community itself had become unhappy over the mental patients and criminals that Fidel Castro had included among the Mariel refugees.[33]

In late September, a political cartoon depicted a speed boat, the *Refugee Policy,* jammed with people, flying the American flag. On top of the boat stood Jimmy Carter, in a naval uniform, and holding the wheel. The wheel was attached to nothing.[34]

The Congress, which had recently passed the Refugee Act, was also attempting to steer American refugee policy. In the House, Representative Elizabeth Holtzman accused the administration of having "no policy for dealing with the current crisis."[35] Representative Holtzman proposed that for asylum seekers already in the United States, those who were eligible for family reunification should be goven regular immigration status; former political prisoners and those who claimed to fear political persecution would have their cases decided individually and would be eligible for federal assistance. These two classes of people fit under the existing immigration and refugee legislation. For all others, Holtzman suggested a special parole.

While the Holtzman plan would have brought some order and consistency to the Mariel inflow, it failed to provide for future mass escapes. In each event, it would have been necessary to parole possibly large numbers of people who would be eligible for neither immigration nor refugee status, thus admitting everyone and limiting only the benefits to which the escapees were entitled.

In the Senate, Edward Kennedy, an author of the 1980 Refugee Act, asserted that the act stipulated that in an unanticipated refugee emergency, such as Mariel, the president had the power, after consultation with Congress, to admit a fixed number of those refugees to the United States. The White House had not applied this provision because it saw the Mariel escapees as asylum seekers, not refugees, since they had come directly to the United States. For this reason, the law did not apply. Kennedy, however, proposed a different interpretation. He argued that although "refugees are arriving directly on our shores, it remains a foreign refugee situation. (A similar situation would arise if Vietnamese 'boat people' reached Guam or Hawaii—as was considered likely in 1978. . . .)" He went on to explain that the Vietnamese would have been given safe haven under the protection of the United Nations High Commissioner for Refugees until permanent resettlement could be arranged, either in the United States or in a third country.[36]

The White House rejected Senator Kennedy's interpretation, but it ought not to have done so. The Kennedy provision recognized what large parts of the country already knew but what Washington chose to ignore, that the United States had already become and would continue to be a destination for many thousands seeking to escape. The critical question was whether, when they reached their destination, it would offer permanent resettlement or only safe haven.

Other senators also recognized the reality outside Washington and spoke to it. Senator Walter Huddleston gave voice to the restrictionists when he said, "We are, deliberately and by inattention, weakening our ability to say 'no' to those who break down our doors by force or by fraud. We have lost control of immigration to this country."[37] Control would quickly become the watchword among politicians.

In the end, the White House proposed neither control nor compassion.

The administration introduced legislation that became the Cuban/Haitian Entrant Act of 1980. The act created a special status for Cubans who had arrived in the United States between April 20 and June 20, 1980, and Haitians who were in INS proceedings before June 20. The Cubans and Haitians covered under the legislation could receive work authorization and the ability to adjust their status to permanent resident after two years. The federal government would reimburse the states for 75 percent of the costs of services to the entrants. The legislation was insufficient. It paid only part of the bill, and it did not pay for all the entrants. The Mariel boatlift did not end until September 26, when Castro shut down the port of Mariel. Representative Dante Fascell of Florida introduced an amendment to the act to provide full reimbursement and refugee-level benefits, including in the Cuban/Haitian Entrant Act all Cubans and Haitians who had arrived in the intervening months. President Carter signed the amendment on October 10, 1980.

Although Washington had failed in its attempt to impose some order on the admission of the Mariel escapees, their admission was only half the problem. The other half was to impose order on their resettlement. In time, order would be imposed, but the early days were a tangle of missteps. The first misstep was the failure of the Immigration and Naturalization Service to adjust its procedures to the new Refugee Act. Accustomed to receiving all Cubans as refugees, the service continued this practice, screening the arriving Cubans briefly, giving each one an application for political asylum, a social security card, and $100 to $150 for immediate expenses, and releasing them into the community. In early May, the service stopped giving out the money when it realized that the Cubans, who came without visas, and whom Congress had not yet approved for refugee admission, were not eligible for the Cuban refugee program.[38] No such embarrassment attached to the Haitian entrants, who were given neither cash nor political asylum forms.

Imposing even the most basic order on the processing of the Cubans required temporary resettlement camps. Tent cities were set up in Miami, first in the Orange Bowl and then under Interstate 95. Then Eglin Air Force Base, in Florida, was pressed into service as a resettlement camp. Amid the chaos of thousands of US Marines, Cuban escapees, and their American relatives, American enterprise broke through; the Cincinnati Red Sox sent scouts to the camp to recruit Cuban baseball players.[39] Although the Cubans were moved out as quickly as sponsors could be found for them, many had no relatives in this country; others were detained because they had criminal records in Cuba that needed to be checked. Like a swelling tide, resettlement camps moved inland from the coast, to Fort Chaffee, Arkansas; Fort Indiantown Gap, Pennsylvania; Fort McCoy, Wisconsin.

Imposing order meant, even more basically, knowing how to process the Cubans. Were they to be admitted under the Cuban refugee program, as applicants for asylum, or as immigrants? If they were not all to be admitted under the Cuban refugee program, what was the disposition for Cubans who did not fit either of the latter two categories? They could not, in any event, be returned to Cuba, since Castro refused to take them back. And what of those Cubans with criminal records found to be inadmissible? Where were they to be detained? Who would assume responsibility for unaccompanied children? Finally, where could sponsors be found for such a large number of people? It would be two months before Washington finally decided to admit all eligible Cubans and Haitians under the Cuban/Haitian Entrant Act.

A second contentious issue was funding and support. In the first chaotic weeks, much of the work of care and screening was undertaken by Cuban volunteers. FEMA assumed responsibility at the end of April, but the White House argued that, since the escapees had not been designated as refugees, they were not entitled to federal assistance. No federal monies were re-leased until May 6, two weeks after the boatlift had begun. Even as late as July and August, voluntary agencies had not been funded. The entrants, ineligible for any federal assistance other than food stamps, became the responsibility of state and local agencies and institutions.[40]

Along with state and local governments, private citizens feared a drain on scarce resources. Workers feared that in time they would lose jobs to the newcomers. The unemployed, however, took some consolation from the temporary jobs that the refugee camps offered. In Fort McCoy, the new camp created 1,500 jobs.[41] In Fort Indiantown Gap, one local businessman boasted, "They've got signs in the employment office for KPs at $5.20 an hour. That's better than dishwashing at the Buck Hotel."[42]

Many of the refugee-processing camps had served the Vietnamese refu-gees just a few years before. But there were major differences between the Vietnamese resettlement effort and this one. The most important difference was that the Vietnamese had been screened and processed before they came to this country. Each Vietnamese refugee who came had a sponsoring agency funded by the federal government. The Cubans arrived without screening, without even the determination that they were entitled to refugee status.

By early May, Havana was putting on board the boats people who had served time in jail. Here it was not known who had been political prisoners and who were common criminals. Nor was it known of the latter what their crimes might have been. One escapee explained, "You can get 20 years for stealing a bottle of rum. Many people are in prison for taking a few beans to feed their families."[43] Some of the arriving Cubans had to be detained in federal prisons; others who had been released to sponsors would commit crimes in this country and be imprisoned later. For still others, sponsorships would break down, and the new arrivals would find themselves homeless.

These were the fringes of an unraveling resettlement effort. But even the fringes had to be gathered up and placed somewhere. As the summer wore on, that somewhere was Fort Chaffee, Arkansas, which became a relocation center for all the hard cases. There were riots and escapes. Authorities found guns and homemade knives, and reported prostitution and drugs. And the people of Arkansas made it very clear that they did not want the Cubans in their state. Governor Bill Clinton lost the election that fall, as did Jimmy Carter. The Mariel boatlift was not kind to politicians.

Around the country the mood of welcome was turning sour. From Miami, Florida, where the first entrants had been received, to Glasgow, Montana, the last site proposed for a resettlement camp, Americans were growing hostile.

As early as mid-May, a Gallup poll found that 59 percent of Americans felt that accepting the Cubans was not good for the country.[44] By late June, nearly 75 percent opposed admitting the Cubans.[45] Polls gave numerical values to the hostility, but the reality lay behind the numbers. Americans voiced concern in four areas. First, and most important, they were concerned that they would lose their jobs to the newcomers. Unemployment had jumped in the last year, and people who had recently lost their jobs or feared that they might lose them were not reassured by assertions that the newcomers were ready to work and contribute to the country. A woman in Arkansas felt, "We should take care of our people at home first. There are enough people here to feed already. It could take employment that we already need—employment for our own people."[46] And in Haltom City, Texas, residents hissed and booed when told that seventy Cuban men had already found jobs in their community. They felt it was unfair to give jobs to Cubans when local residents were unemployed.[47] The most vulnerable, and often the most voluble, were those earning the lowest wages.

A second fear was also economic. Americans worried that if the escapees did not find work, they would receive welfare or social security. They would also increase demands on overburdened hospitals, schools, and other social services, raising taxes for everyone. Such fears were only exacerbated by news reports that Cubans arriving in Florida were handed social security cards along with their applications for political asylum. A Wichita man asked, "Why should we, as United States citizens, have our tax money used to defray expenses for these immigrants? . . . In the United States, there are many citizens out of work. Much of our tax money is needed for US citizens. . . . We should help our own people above everybody else."[48]

An Arizona woman said simply, "We are not the world's police force, nor welfare agency." Another asked, "When the working citizen is no longer working, who is going to take care of everyone?"[49]

News reports fed a third fear, that Castro was emptying his jails and mental hospitals and depositing their inmates on the boats headed for the United States. In Fort Indiantown Gap, Pennsylvania, a waitress said she didn't "mind people who need a home coming here, but they're talking about criminals being mixed in." She confessed to being "scared" and wanted to know "what kind of security they'll have to prevent them from coming down into the towns."[50] Many residents of the town apparently took responsibility for their own security; the county district attorney, learning that citizens were arming themselves, urged them not to use deadly force against fleeing Cubans.[51] A Texas woman said she had been told to "lock all the windows and doors and not to let the children play outside after dark without supervision."[52] A paranoid underside of the American psyche was being revealed.

The fourth area of concern was not a fear at all but simply restrictionism. The restrictionists, cutting their arguments from the current economic cloth, acknowledged that when their parents and grandparents had come, America needed immigrants, needed their labor, but it did not need immigrants any more. A man in Edwardsville, Illinois, wrote, "We no longer live in the late 1800s or early 1900s. . . . Many more workers were needed and immigrants were welcomed to the United States. All that has changed. Now there is unemployment. Yet we have for many years continued to permit foreigners to enter our country, knowing full well our own workers cannot easily find jobs."[53] A New York woman seemed to agree. She wrote, "Yes, the myth goes, we are all immigrants, . . . [but] earlier immigrants came to a young, sprawling, growing country that needed lots of farmers and semi-skilled laborers. Modern America has few farmers and even fewer semi-skilled or unskilled jobs—not even enough for those who are already here."[54] At times restrictionism descended to raw prejudice. Some declared the new-comers to be hardly more than savages. The Ku Klux Klan flew its banner over a refugee camp in Florida[55] and joined residents at a city council meeting in Texas to protest the resettlement of 138 Cuban refugees in their community.[56]

But even during the height of the clamor, some Americans were arguing quietly and simply for other options. One such option was presented in a letter to the *Washington Post.* Louis Gershenow, of Bowie, Maryland, asked:

> Would it not be more feasible and in the better interest of our country to require that additional refugees from Cuba be taken to Guantánamo Naval

Station for processing prior to permitting them to arrive in the United States? I believe it would also be in the best interests and safety of the refugees.

Many of the logistical problems of housing, food, medical attention and sanitation could be provided by large troop transports anchored in the harbor. The undesirables screened out could more easily be returned from whence they came.

The suggestion, I think, would provide for a more orderly and less risky undertaking and would alleviate the heavy load on and adverse criticism of the present holding and processing facilities.[57]

Screening the escapees on Guantánamo would have achieved several other ends. First, it would have deprived Castro of his tactical advantage, of his ability to visit embarrassment and turmoil on the United States. This, in turn, would have enabled the United States to engage him in negotiations. Second, the criminals and other undesirables would not have entered this country, eliminating a major cause of the public backlash. That backlash could have been further ameliorated with Cubans and Haitians being resettled in a well-paced and orderly manner.

But the quiet voices were lost in the din of "adverse criticism." The single largest concern was economic, the fear of losing jobs, of additional burdensome taxes. Americans' concerns over jobs and taxes were legitimate. These concerns needed to be addressed. They were not. The government had badly mismanaged the Mariel boatlift, not only by failing to impose some order on the boatlift itself, but also in failing to assist the local communities. The mismanagement of Mariel had cast a shadow over the country. And in that shadow fear grew to anger, anger fed prejudice, and prejudice demanded a voice in politics. The Mariel boatlift receded in memory, but the anger and prejudice remained. They resurface periodically, directed against other groups perceived as gate crashers—asylum seekers, undocumented workers, non-English speakers.

The Mariel boatlift lent a spurious legitimacy to American restrictionism, a restrictionism that would infect not only domestic but also foreign policy. Foreign policy decisions, as we shall see, would now invoke the fear of "hordes of refugees" as their justification. President Reagan, and Bush after him, invoked support for their anticommunist Central American policies with the threat that only support for those actions could prevent or stem refugee movements. By 1994, under President Clinton, preventing refugee flows had come to mean not ameliorating the conditions that led to their creation, but confining the refugees to the place of their oppression.

Domestically, the watchword was control. Immigrants, refugees, asylum seekers, illegal entrants, all were lumped together in the public mind as opportunists trying to defraud a system that was "out of control." Election campaigns from the local to the presidential level would sound the alarm that Americans had lost control, were losing their country—to crime, to welfare, and to immigration. And the Mariel boatlift had come to symbolize all three.

The Mariel boatlift had ended, but a new era had begun, the era of exclusion. Although the boatlift ended abruptly when Fidel Castro shut down the port of Mariel, the era of exclusion would arrive incrementally. We would again systematically obstruct Haitians, and even though we would continue to accept Cubans who arrived on our shores, a subtle form of exclusion had begun even for them. After Camarioca, we had instituted freedom flights from Cuba; after Mariel, there was no such orderly escape route. The only option available would be the risky one of illicit departure by boat. In 1994, Cuban emigrants would find even that passage closed to them, as the United States, as it had done to the Haitians before them, interdicted the Cubans and barred them from escape.

Through the decades of the eighties and nineties, the United States would, in a campaign to regain control of our borders, gradually push those borders back. By 1994, the borders we were seeking to control were the borders of many refugee-producing countries. In the next chapter, we will trace the competing pressures of the period. On the one side were the churches, the courts, and the citizens who argued for equity and fairness. On the other side were the government, the bureaucracy, and the citizens who argued for restriction and exclusion. By 1994, the exclusionists had won.

After the Mariel boatlift had ended, presidential assistant Jack Watson conceded that the administration had done nothing to prevent another Mariel. "This is certainly a problem that we are going to have to face," he said. "It is going to remain a serious problem for the remainder of this decade."[58] Watson was only partly correct; the problem is one we will have to face into the next century. Not the problem of Mariel in the narrowest sense, of preventing sudden mass escapes, but the problem of Mariel in the widest sense—of how the United States, as a country grounded in law and freedom, will respond to those individuals who have been denied both.

4
Erecting Floodgates: Escape by Sea

The numbers of Haitians asking asylum in the United States were relatively small. Yet to the Justice Department, the Haitian asylum seekers were a massive cloud looming on the southeastern horizon. At a closed, high-level meeting of the Immigration and Naturalization Service in 1978, Deputy Commissioner Mario Noto gave the order to "ACTUALLY PAIN [*sic*] OUT THE DIMENSIONS OF THE HAITIAN THREAT.... Volatile— show that these are unusual cases dealing with individuals that are threatening the community's well-being—socially and economically."[1] The capital letters in which his opening statement was transcribed convey the force of Noto's conviction.

Thus began the Immigration Service's Haitian Program, a deliberate effort to expel Haitians from the Miami area and to discourage other Haitians from coming to the United States. Two years later, Judge James Lawrence King would state,"Those Haitians who came to the United States seeking freedom and justice did not find it. Instead, they were confronted with an Immigration and Naturalization Service determined to deport them. The decision was made among high INS officials to expel Haitians, despite whatever claims to asylum individual Haitians might have. A Program was set up to accomplish this goal."[2]

Judge King ordered the Immigration Service to rehear all the Haitian asylum claims that it had rejected. New hearings could be ordered; a new state of mind could not. One year after Judge King's order, a spokesman for the Immigration and Naturalization Service explained his mindset: "What I keep in mind is that these are illegal aliens, just like Germans or French or any other nationality would be if they tried to enter this country without the proper documents."[3]

American policy makers and bureaucrats could fear the Haitians as a sinister threat to the community, or they could dismiss them as opportunistic, illegal aliens attempting to circumvent our immigration laws. But both views ignored the reality. Haitians were escaping, in increasing numbers, from widespread repression and random persecution. And the United States was unprepared for mass escape. In addition to immigration, there were three legal avenues by which those who fled their countries could gain entry to ours: as refugees, as members of a group given parole, or as asylum seekers. The government had never opened the first two avenues—refugee status and parole—to Haitians and made every effort to close the third—asylum.

The Haitians were not eligible for admission as refugees. Each year, the executive and the Congress determine which countries will be designated for refugee admissions and apportion the year's refugee numbers among those countries. Nowhere does the troika of interests run more freely than here. Foreign policy determines which countries will be eligible for refugee admissions. Domestic pressures and the costs of resettlement help to determine how many will be processed from each of those countries. Haiti's dictators were friends of the United States, allies in the campaign against Fidel Castro. Foreign policy would not be served by calling attention to Haiti's human rights abuses. Therefore, no refugee numbers were allocated to Haiti.

Parole was another avenue closed to the Haitians, although it had been freely opened to the Cubans. From 1962 until Mariel in 1980, the nearly 700,000 Cubans who were admitted to the United States entered under a parole—admission to the United States outside normal immigration channels. The 1978 program to admit former Cuban political prisoners to the United States was a parole program. Although the Refugee Act of 1980 terminated the attorney general's parole power, the Cuban-Haitian Entrant Act that followed Mariel was in fact a parole by Congress. But it is unlikely that Haitians, had they not been swept in with the Cubans, would ever have been given parole. No less than refugee allocations, the parole power rode behind the troika of interests.

Foreclosed from applying for refugee admission, ignored as recipients of parole, the Haitians had only one avenue remaining—to flee their country illegally and ask for asylum in the United States. In every respect, this avenue was by far the most treacherous. An individual who comes to the United States and asks to be given asylum must prove that she has a well-founded fear of being persecuted in her country of origin. Applying for asylum is a difficult and time-consuming, case-by-case process. Asylum was not designed as an avenue wide enough to accommodate masses of people.

When large numbers of people escape their country in a short period of time, there is no distinct avenue for them to travel. Neither with the passage of the Refugee Act in 1980 nor at present has any such avenue been planned. The Refugee Act of 1980 had been impelled, in part, by the needs of a mass movement of refugees—the Southeast Asians who were the living casualties of the Vietnam War. Behind the Southeast Asians lay adumbrations of other groups in flight—the Jews of World War II, the Hungarians, émigrés from the Soviet Union. With these refugees in mind, the authors of the Refugee Act planned for every foreseeable aspect of the admission and resettlement of refugees from overseas. The members of Congress, however, focused as they were on refugees abroad, had failed to provide for the admission and resettlement of asylum seekers, individuals coming directly to the United States and asking to be given safe haven; only at the urging of the United Nations High Commissioner for Refugees was asylum included in the act. Provisions were added to allow the attorney general to grant asylum to individuals and to allow, each year, up to five thousand of those asylees to become permanent residents, the first step to citizenship.

Five thousand. A generous number since fewer than one thousand grants of asylum were being made each year. But within six weeks of the passage of the Refugee Act, Fidel Castro had opened the port of Mariel and more than 75,000 Cubans had escaped to South Florida. Six months later, the United States was attempting to resettle nearly 125,000 Cubans and over 15,000 Haitians. No longer concerned with seemingly generous asylum numbers, the United States was now beset by what it thought of as *mass* asylum.

In fact, the Cubans and Haitians who swept the Florida shores in the spring and summer of 1980, like the Central Americans who would shortly press across the southwestern border, should have been seen not as a mass asylum but rather as what could be called a mass escape. To claim asylum, an individual must show that she or he has a well-founded fear of persecution because of race, religion, nationality, membership in a particular social group, or political opinion. Mass asylum applies to large numbers of people with some common basis for fearing such persecution. The humanitarian response, in such cases, would be to determine that the entire group is entitled to refugee status and resettlement.

But the Mariel Cubans and Haitians were not a single entity and did not all fear persecution. Considered individually, many Cubans and Haitians could demonstrate a well-founded fear of persecution and would, therefore, have been eligible for refugee status. But there were others who could not prove such a fear; even these, however, had had their freedom restricted, had been oppressed, even if they had not been persecuted. The Cubans and Haitians did not, as a whole, represent either mass asylum or an undocumented labor migration. (The State Department generally likened the Haitians to Mexicans, but this was a willful distortion of their situation.) They represented the phenomenon of mass escape, a phenomenon not envisioned in our immigration laws, nor responded to by our lawmakers.

For many years, the government had been responding to Cubans and Haitians in disparate but politically determined ways. When Cubans arrived on our shores, they were nearly always judged to be political refugees; Haitians were nearly always judged to be economic migrants. Neither country can be said to have enjoyed the freedoms of democracy, but Cuba and Haiti denied those freedoms differently. In Cuba, authority stemmed from the central government and was rigidly enforced. In Haiti, authority was delegated through the civilian security forces and was arbitrarily translated into terror and extortion. Whatever their individual motives for seeking asylum, when they reached our shores, Cubans and Haitians were treated as groups. Cubans were accepted as political refugees and given resettlement assistance; Haitians were rejected as economic migrants and placed in deportation or exclusion proceedings.

The very concept of "mass asylum" begs an important question. If any single country is forcing masses of its citizens to flee, and large numbers of those people then request asylum, clearly there is some basis for giving that country a refugee allocation. The "mass asylum" that we feared was, in a real sense, our own creation. The United States ignored the repression in Haiti, refused to process refugees from there, failed to give fair asylum hearings to Haitian escapees, and eventually barred them even from leaving their country, all the while staring with unseeing eyes at the egregious abuses of human rights that were driving them out.

For the United States, human rights abuses in another country have never been the primary reason to accept its refugees or asylum seekers. At best, human rights abuses lend additional weight to what remains inherently a foreign policy decision. Mark Gibney and Michael Stohl have compared the human rights conditions in scores of countries with the United States' acceptance of refugees and asylum seekers. The countries were given yearly rankings from 1 to 5 to indicate "the level of political violence and terror that country experiences."[4] Levels 1 and 2 indicate rare or low levels of human rights abuse. At Level 3, "There is extensive political imprisonment. . . . Execution or other political murders and brutality may be common. Unlimited detention, with or without trial, for political views is accepted. . . . " At Level 4, "Murders, disappearances, and torture are a common part of life. . . ." At Level 5, the entire population is subjected to terror.[5] Haiti, in 1980, was ranked Level 4 using the human rights reports of Amnesty International, and Level 3 using reports of the US Department of State. Cuba, in that same year was ranked 3 in both reports.

When these rankings were then compared with US refugee admissions,

Gibney and Stohl made a remarkable discovery. They found, "US refugee policy shows little relationship to the level of human rights conditions in other countries. In fact, it is safe to say that refugee admissions is the special preserve of individuals from Level 3 countries, rather than Levels 4 or 5." In 1980, for example, the year in which the Refugee Act was passed, more than 84 percent of refugee admissions were from Level 3 countries, while *only 4 percent* of the total were from Level 4 and 5 countries.[6] No refugees were admitted from Haiti, a Level 4 country, until 1992, when the United States accepted fifty-four Haitians as refugees.[7]

Although the United States was compelled to acknowledge the flagrant human rights abuses in Haiti, it needed also to offer some reasons why these abuses did not make Haitians eligible for refugee status or asylum. Two reasons were given. The most frequently cited reason involved a certain sleight of hand. With one hand, the government would demonstrate that Haiti was indeed a repressive country. But that hand would be stealthily withdrawn while the other hand presented evidence of severe poverty in Haiti. For the rest of the presentation, repression in Haiti was hidden. Rather, the argument would be made that, in the words of John A. Bushnell, deputy assistant secretary for inter-American affairs, "The stark contrast between living conditions and economic prospects in Haiti and the United States is the principal factor motivating emigration to this country."[8] Allied to the idea that the Haitians fled poverty, not persecution, that Haitians were, in essence, illegal entrants, came the next argument. "Unlike Cuba, the Haitian Government has permitted emigration—documented or not—to proceed freely."[9] We ignored the human rights abuses in Haiti, since human rights had never been the driving force behind our refugee policy. And we focused instead on economics, the economic deprivation in Haiti, the economic threat to the United States.

The Haitian boat people had been coming to the United States since 1972, when the first escapees from Duvalier's prisons washed up on the Florida shore. They had been coming to the United States in waves, in rhythm with the waves of repression in Haiti. The numbers of Haitians had never been large, but their significance had always been larger than their numbers. To the American public, the Haitians were a threat to a weak economy; to the American government, the Haitians were a threat to a weak border control.

These perceived threats have formed the rationale for the United States' entire policy toward the Haitian asylum seekers. From the early, and clumsy, attempts of the INS to deny work authorizations to Haitian asylum seekers, through detaining them and denying them the protection of law, to the interdiction of Haitians on the high seas and their forcible return to

Haiti, the entire policy was grounded in one simple premise: Haitians are seeking jobs in the United States and they must be prevented from doing so.

The Haitians occupy a unique place in American refugee history. They were the first nationality to seek asylum (rather than the refugee status or parole that were not available to them) in significant numbers. In FY 1980 the INS granted asylum to two Haitians, in FY 1981 to five.[10] They were also the first group about whom the government made a policy decision, not only to deny asylum, but also to discourage and deter those who would apply for it. The Haitians were the first, but they would not be the last. The US government would later apply the methods used against the Haitians to other unwanted groups of asylum seekers, such as the Central Americans. And other refugee-receiving countries would use those same methods against their unwanted asylum seekers, citing as precedent the United States' treatment of the Haitians. When, for example, Hong Kong began the forcible return of Vietnamese boat people, its defense was that it was applying the same policy that the United States had applied to the Haitians.

That policy—to deter Haitians from seeking asylum in the United States—reached its overt climax in 1994, with the White House decision to deploy troops to Haiti. The policy began, in 1978, with covert meetings of high-level personnel from the INS and Justice and State departments. The purpose of these meetings was to devise a program to expel Haitians from South Florida rapidly and without impediment and to discourage other Haitians from coming to the United States.

For the Haitians already in South Florida, expulsion seemed the only option available to the Immigration Service. It had already tried to hold in jail all Haitians who asked for political asylum. When the jails became overcrowded, however, Haitians had to be released on bond. Unrelenting, the INS refused to give work authorizations to the released Haitians. The asylum seekers crowded together in substandard housing, with one or two "legal" Haitian wage earners who paid the rent. There was soon widespread starvation in the Haitian community. The National Council of Churches brought suit against the Justice Department on behalf of the Haitians, asserting that they were refugees seeking asylum under the United Nations Convention on Refugees, which granted the right to be released from jail and to work. The case was appealed all the way to the Supreme Court, attracting much public attention along the way. While the case was still before the Court, the government capitulated and the INS agreed to give work authorizations to any Haitian whose asylum request was in process.

But the INS mistakenly broadcast the message in Florida that *any* Haitian (not only those with asylum claims in process) who presented himself to the INS office would be given a work permit. Three thousand Haitians came out of hiding, applied for, and were given work authorizations. At the same time, Washington was receiving reports that the Bahamas planned to expel some 40,000 Haitians who had taken refuge there; many of them could be expected shortly to make their way to Florida. Ignoring the legal agreement, Washington ordered the INS to revoke all work authorizations and to issue no others.

Stronger measures were needed. A high-level meeting was called to discuss how the United States should proceed in three areas: detaining Haitian asylum seekers in the United States, denying them due process in the adjudication of their asylum claims, and deterring future asylum seekers from Haiti. A plan was devised that came to be known as the Haitian Program.

The first step in the Haitian Program was an order to incarcerate all Haitian males. In contravention of the agreement with the National Council of Churches, they were not to be released on bond nor to be given work authorizations. But a far more invidious step was to follow. In order to reject Haitian asylum claims and deport the Haitians as quickly as possible, the government abruptly put a new policy into place. Haitian asylum applicants were not to be informed that they had a right to ask asylum or that they had a right to counsel. In order to speed up the proceedings, Deputy INS Commissioner Mario Noto called for more immigration judges, more courtroom space, and he asked the immigration judges to triple the number of cases they heard. He recommended that they conduct "MASH-type" hearings, in which groups of Haitians had their asylum claims heard and decided en masse.[11] The advisory opinions of the State Department's Bureau of Human Rights and Humanitarian Affairs were reduced to form letters.

The most critical and delicate aspect of the asylum process is the interview. It is the interviewer who first decides whether the refugee is to be believed. Refugees are often fearful of questioning and unable to offer documentation for their claims. The interviewer, therefore, must be skillful and sensitive if he is to elicit information from the refugee. Yet in its pressure to expel the Haitians, the INS engaged airport inspectors as interviewers. If an applicant was forthcoming and did offer lengthy testimony on her fear of persecution, Creole translators would abbreviate her statement to just a few words, or even substitute the words, "I came to find work."

It is often very difficult for the asylum applicant to provide evidence to support her claim. This important task is usually carried out by counsel. An experienced attorney may need from ten to forty hours to assemble the necessary documents for each client. The INS allowed the pro bono attorneys thirty to sixty minutes. The attorneys were not only pressured but harassed and threatened by INS officials. An almost farcical strategy was to schedule the attorneys for several hearings, sometimes as many as fifteen or twenty, in different buildings. In one case, a lawyer, dashing from one hearing to another, was berated by the immigration judge for his lateness.[12]

The immigration judges were also being pressured. A normal caseload would have been about 5 cases a day. Under the Haitian Program, each judge was expected to hear 100 a day, even, at one point, 150. The judges were not to "hear" the cases, but only to hand down a decision—to deny asylum. In that four-month period from August to November of 1978, the immigration judges heard and denied approximately 4,000 applications for asylum.

In the fall of 1978, a group of pro bono attorneys, acting on behalf of the Haitian Refugee Center in Miami and Haitian asylum applicants, obtained a temporary restraining order from the district court in southern Florida. The order enjoined the attorney general from continuing the accelerated hearings and from returning to Haiti those Haitians whose asylum claims had been denied.[13] In the spring of 1980, as the Mariel boatlift was beginning, the class action suit, *Haitian Refugee Center v. Civiletti,* was being argued. Attorneys for the Haitians intended to show that the government had acted illegally, violating both United States immigration law and INS regulations. Now the government was on the defensive, but it offered little defense. Arguments presented by attorneys for the Justice Department seemed almost desultory; Judge James Lawrence King commented that "most of the defendants, the main defendants, have washed their hands of the suit."[14]

Judge King, a Republican appointed by President Nixon, found for the plaintiffs. He wrote: "The plaintiffs charge that they faced a transparently discriminatory program designed to deport Haitian nationals and no one else. The uncontroverted evidence proves their claim."[15] He went on, "This Program, in its planning and executing, is offensive to every notion of constitutional due process and equal protection. The Haitians whose claims for asylum were rejected during the Program shall not be deported until they are given a fair chance to present their claims for political asylum."[16]

If the government had had little interest in battling the Haitians in a court of law, it might have been because it had already decided to battle them in the field. The government appealed Judge King's ruling, but at the same time acted to remove newly arriving Haitians from the court's jurisdiction. Newly arriving Haitians would be processed not in South Florida but in Puerto Rico. In Puerto Rico, Haitians not only were beyond the reach of the district court, they were also beyond the help of pro bono attorneys and support groups. They would be isolated and vulnerable.

In the months that followed, the INS took detained Haitians from Miami, where they had legal representatives, to Puerto Rico, where they had none. Attorneys came to the detention camp to meet with their clients only to find them gone. Family members of the Haitian detainees were not able to trace them. Many had been quietly sent back to Haiti.

The Haitian Program in South Florida and its reincarnation in Puerto Rico reveal a crude chasm between the rhetoric and the reality of American refugee policy. Neither the rhetoric nor the reality changes, no matter which party is in power. The rhetoric had been intoned by President Jimmy Carter during the Mariel boatlift; it would be repeated by candidate Ronald Reagan in his acceptance of the Republican nomination:

> Can we doubt that only a divine Providence placed this land, this land of freedom, here as a refuge for all those people in the world who yearn to breathe free? Jews and Christians enduring persecution behind the Iron Curtain, the boat people of Southeast Asia, Cuba, and Haiti.[17]

Ronald Reagan spoke compassionately; but, like others before him, when he became president, he carried a big stick. Reagan had a mandate to achieve several goals: to reestablish the United States as a world power, to revive the economy, and to restore law and order. The Reagan administration quickly realized that a nation that controlled its borders was saying to the world that it brooked no violations of its sovereignty, that it would return American jobs to American workers, and that it would not only enforce the immigration laws but protect Americans from lawbreakers.

The control of American borders served not only domestic policy but foreign policy as well. Control could be selective: escapees from communist countries would be welcomed, paraded as symbols of the American commitment to freedom; escapees from noncommunist countries would be turned away, displayed as symbols of the administration's commitment to the expulsion of gate crashers. It became a truism of the Reagan administration philosophy that, in the words of Eugene Douglas, the United States coordinator for refugee affairs, "the tyrannies spawning refugees today all bear the Marxist-Leninist label."[18] Haitians, who, unlike the Cubans, did not come from a "Marxist-Leninist" tyranny, were not "legally eligible for refugee status as a group."[19]

President Reagan appointed his own Task Force on Immigration and Refugee Policy, a cabinet-level committee chaired by the attorney general. The deliberations of the Reagan Task Force were disproportionately concerned with keeping out the Haitians. The task force acknowledged that for the previous decade 35,000 Haitians were estimated to have arrived in the United States, as compared to 130,000 Cubans; moreover, Haitians were less than 2 percent of the total undocumented immigration to the United States. Yet the task force turned much of its attention and directed many of its recommendations to the exclusion of the Haitian asylum seekers. Why were Haitians so singled out?

Many advocates for the Haitians argue that they were the targets of racism. Certainly racism has played a part in American restrictionism. But at a government level, there was a more pressing concern—the fear of another Mariel. Almost every government spokesperson and every government report raises that fear. The fear of a sudden flood of refugees, however, had to be given a larger justification and was placed in the context of anticommunist dogma. The government position was well expressed by Thomas O. Enders, assistant secretary of state for inter-American affairs, who argued that "a sudden massive outflow of tens of thousands of people in a very short period of time . . . can occur only in a totalitarian state." From Haiti, on the other hand, migration was a "matter of choice." Enders went on:

> In one case we are dealing with a friendly government which is interested in enforcing its laws and respectful of the laws of its neighbors and wishes to cooperate with the United States in bringing illegal migration under control, and migration occurs as a result of individual decisions without the support or the sanction of the Government. In the other case, such as in the Mariel boatlift of last year, we had a deliberate decision by the Cuban Government to permit and in many cases to force the departure of large numbers of its citizens to the United States.[20]

Government policy makers had succeeded, rhetorically at least, in reducing refugee movements to immigration concerns. Mass escape arose not from the absence of freedom but from the absence of immigration controls. This line of reasoning lent still another area of support to our anti-Cuba, pro-Haiti bias: A hostile Castro was manipulating emigration; an amicable Duvalier was agreeable to containing it. A corollary to this argument was that Castro refused to take back Cubans returned from the United States, while Duvalier agreed to take back Haitians. Therefore, the United States could not send back Cuban asylum seekers, but it could deport Haitians. Lost in the permutations of foreign policy was the most basic question: Were the Cubans and Haitians escaping because of a well-founded fear of persecution?

The government's policy, however, was not based exclusively on rigid anticommunism. The Reagan administration was also under pressure from Florida's governor and congressional delegation to stop the flow of asylum seekers into the state. The flow of asylum seekers, to a Florida politician, meant Haitians, not Cubans. The politically powerful Cuban-American community would not brook even the suggestion that Cubans might be turned away. If the Cubans could not be stopped, the Haitians must be.

President Reagan's Immigration Task Force had not been appointed to deal with questions of asylum. From the first, its task was to establish a United States policy toward "foreign persons who enter south Florida without visas."[21] Haitians, as a group, had been reduced from asylum seekers to illegal entrants. All were lawbreakers who must be stopped, while the INS was a law enforcer that must be strengthened. The task force looked at the judicially discredited Haitian Program from the opposite side of the looking glass. In its view, "The Immigration and Naturalization Service attempted to expedite deportation determinations for Haitians within the limits of the statutorily prescribed hearing process."[22] It took note of the ruling enjoining the INS from deporting Haitians, but reasoned that, since Judge King's order applied only to Haitians who had applied for asylum *before* May 9, 1979, it was permissible to deport *newly* arriving Haitians.

The task force considered three options for excluding Haitians: interdiction at sea, detention, and "procedural reform." Procedural reform was a euphemism for denying the Haitians due process. Procedures were reformed almost immediately. By June of 1981, mass hearings were again being held. Asylum hearings were scheduled for thirty Haitians at a time, in locked courtrooms, from which pro bono attorneys were barred. The Haitian Program of 1978 was being reenacted, and its script had been written by President Reagan's Task Force in collaboration with the highest-ranking officials of the Justice Department and the INS; some of them had been the architects of the first Haitian Program. The National Emergency Civil Liberties Committee sued, and a temporary restraining order was issued.[23]

A second option considered by the task force was detention. Detention, it felt, could be a deterrent to Haitian migration, "especially if expulsion from the United States were to occur expeditiously."[24] On July 30, 1981, President Reagan and his attorney general announced a policy to "detain undocumented aliens" who were in exclusion proceedings. The undocumented aliens who were detained would be preponderantly Haitians. When suit was brought, in *Louis v. Nelson,* to challenge the legality of the second Haitian Program, the plaintiffs introduced statistical evidence of the INS's discriminatory detention practices. One statistician, comparing the data on Haitians who had been detained to that on non-Haitians who had been paroled, described the difference as so great as to be a "statistical joke." The evidence proved that, overwhelmingly, entrants were detained not because they came without documentation but because they were Haitian.[25]

Although detention would be costly, the task force also argued that it could "relieve some of the tensions created by release of visaless aliens into the community."[26] Not only did the INS incur greater costs when it held the Haitians in detention, the service also found itself unable to provide them with "basic amenities and services." "The housing and services provided to the Haitian detainees were," according to a government report, "unsuitable for lengthy detention" and "did not meet long term needs."[27] When the government restored its policy of imprisoning Haitian asylum seekers, it also restored another practice. Just as it had previously spirited Haitians from the detention camp in South Florida to a camp in Puerto Rico, it now began removing Haitians with legal representation from South Florida to distant areas of the country where no pro bono counsel was available. By the time suit was brought in *Louis v. Nelson,* 2,100 Haitians had been dispersed around the country. Once again, the court enjoined the INS from transferring Haitians away from their attorneys. The Justice Department, however, refused to provide the court with the names and locations of all the Haitians affected by the suit. The irate judge accused the department of "playing [a] human shell game."[28]

On June 18, 1982, the district court for southern Florida ruled against the INS and nullified its detention policy. The INS appealed the ruling, and protested that unless it could immediately reinstate its detention policy, the United States faced a "potential emergency." The emergency had been detailed by the governor of Florida, Bob Graham: "There are between 20,000 and 40,000 Haitians in the Bahamas as well as additional numbers of Haitians, Nicaraguans, El Salvadorans and other nationals currently residing in other areas within the Caribbean basin.... [The governor] fears a renewed influx of Haitian and other aliens into south Florida if the court's judgment . . . is not stayed."[29]

Governor Graham, along with Florida's congressional representatives, was strongly pressuring the federal government to cut off the flow of émigrés from Haiti. The Immigration Task Force concluded that the most effective means was to cut off that flow before it ever reached the United States. Haitian boats could be intercepted in the waters off Haiti, a swift determination made whether any on board were entitled to asylum hearings, and all others returned to Haiti. The task force saw many advantages to interdiction at sea. Most obviously, it would deter migration. Would-be émigrés, realizing that they would be quickly intercepted and returned to Haiti, would be discouraged from taking to the seas. As a result, those same Haitians would be kept out of "administrative and judicial proceedings in the United States."[30] thereby reducing the necessity and costs of detention as well as of asylum hearings.

The Convention relating to the Status of Refugees, which the United States has signed, as referred to earlier, states:

No contracting State shall expel or return ("refouler") a refugee in any manner whatsoever to the frontiers of territories where his life or freedom would be
threatened on account of his race religion, nationality, membership of a particular
social group or political opinion.[31]

The task force acknowledged that the United States, as a signatory to the
United Nations protocol, was required to hear "refugee claims prior to
returning a claimant to his homeland." It argued, however, that the United
States Immigration Act, which executed the convention, did not apply outside of US territorial waters.[32] By this reasoning, then, it would be possible
to return Haitians without even determining whether they had a well-
founded fear of persecution.

If the task force was untroubled by ethical considerations, it did acknowledge some more practical disadvantages. First was the cost. The task
force estimated a cost of between $10 and $15 million a year. (In fact, by
1984, the cost for the Coast Guard alone had reached $25 million a year;
1,900 Haitians had been interdicted at a cost of $36,000 per Haitian sent
back to Haiti.[33]) A second disadvantage was that it would divert the Coast
Guard from its other responsibilities, such as intercepting drug smugglers.
And finally, there was the danger that some Haitians might resist being
returned to Haiti, requiring the Coast Guard to use deadly force.

The task force also considered that interdiction might create some delicate problems for foreign policy. The United States was pressing the Southeast Asian countries to continue to offer first asylum to Indochinese boat
refugees. It was recommended that the State Department explain that there
was a crucial distinction between the Haitians and the Indochinese: the
Haitian government was willing to take back any returned refugees. It was
also feared that Black Caribbean and African nations might perceive the
interdiction policy as racist. To these countries too, the State Department
would offer explanations. What these explanations might be was never
elaborated. Never mentioned was the Jackson-Vanik Amendment, enacted
in 1974, which denied most-favored-nation status to countries that restricted
or taxed the emigration of their citizens. As the task force was completing
its deliberations, Senator Lawton Chiles, a Florida Democrat, demanded
immediate action. "We need a decision from the White House," he said,
"that they're going to interdict the boats, that they're going to stop the
flow." And, Chiles went on, Haitians intercepted at sea "don't have to have
due process. They can simply be sent back to Haiti willy-nilly by the Coast
Guard."[34] The outspoken Senator Chiles would soon have his way.

On September 23, 1981, the United States entered into an agreement
with the Duvalier government "to stop the clandestine migration of numer-
ous residents of Haiti to the United States and to the mutual desire of our

two countries to cooperate to stop such illegal migration." The two governments agreed to "the establishment of a cooperative program of interdiction
and selective return to Haiti of certain Haitian migrants and vessels involved in illegal transport of persons coming from Haiti."[35] The United
States Coast Guard would patrol the open waters off Haiti, stop and board
Haitian boats, and return to Haiti any Haitians who lacked exit visas. On
board the Coast Guard ships were to be INS officers whose task was to
determine if any Haitian on board should be brought to the United States for
an asylum hearing.[36] Also on board would be a Haitian naval officer.

The interdiction agreement wore two faces. Turned toward Haiti, the
face was resolute and brooked no resistance. The American ambassador to
Haiti issued a statement:

> We regret that we cannot receive all people from other countries desiring to
> live in the United States. Unfortunately, such an inflow would be highly
> disruptive to the economic and social structure of our country. I therefore
> wish to convey clearly to the country of Haiti that those who contemplate
> paying large sums of money to traffickers to take them to the United States . . .
> will lose their money to traffickers and end up back in Haiti. . . . [37]

Turned toward the United States, the face was benevolent. The interdiction of Haitian boats on the high seas would be a life-saving mission. After
thirty-three Haitians drowned off the coast of Florida, Senator Lawton
Chiles commiserated:

> I think it's a tragedy. And the only way I think we're going to stop it is to
> increase the presence out there and interdict some of the boats and take them
> back. Then I think people will quit selling their farms, quit paying the money
> and then I think we have a chance to stop the loss of lives that [is] coming
> from these unseaworthy craft. These smugglers that are getting people on
> these boats are charging $1,000 apiece for people to go. They tell them that
> the streets in the United States are lined with gold or coins . . . and that's a
> tragedy that they're putting them on these boats that way.[38]

The first boat was interdicted by the Coast Guard in late October. Both
sides saw their positions vindicated. For the law-and-order advocates, fifty-
six Haitians had been kept out of the United States; not one had been
brought here to request political asylum. The kind-hearted were relieved
that all had been saved from tragic death on a sinking boat. The boat was
named the *Exoribe,* the exodus.

The interdiction agreement elicited strong criticism, not only from civil
libertarians and Haitian advocates, but also from newspapers in Florida and
around the country. The *Miami News,* criticizing as well the Reagan deten-

tion policy, ran a piece, "Haitian Interdiction Blemish on America," which
said:

> The US Government is so accommodating to its hemispheric neighbors that
> very soon Haitians will no longer have to come to these shores to participate
> in American-style justice with its prison camps, its furtive nighttime depar-
> tures for Puerto Rico, its threats of incarceration in Glasgow, Montana, where
> the temperature dropped to 28 last week.
> Soon American-style justice will float out to the international waters be-
> tween Cuba and Haiti in the form of Coast Guard cutters staffed with asylum
> officers to shuffle the Haitians through quasi-courtrooms before shunting
> them back to poverty and oppression they fled.[39]

The *Miami Herald* headlined "Poor Excuse for Policy: Stopping Haitian
Boats," and wondered if the Coast Guard "would open fire on a vessel
carrying civilians, including children?"[40] The *New York Times* questioned
the administration's "principle and consistency." Why interdict Haitians
fleeing persecution when the United States was not interdicting a far larger
number of undocumented Mexicans who were coming in search of work?[41]
And for those who watched both Haitian and Cuban arrivals, the disparity
in treatment was painful.

By 1991, when Haitian President Jean-Bertrand Aristide was overthrown, the Coast Guard had intercepted 443 boats and returned them to
Haiti; 23,551 Haitians had been interdicted, of whom 28 had been taken to
the United States and permitted to apply for asylum.[42]

It is likely that some of the other 23,523 Haitians had been too inarticu-
late or simply too frightened to explain their need for asylum. The Lawyers
Committee for Human Rights, in 1989, searched out and spoke with some
of the returned Haitians. Mr. Alexis was one of them. A schoolteacher, he
had headed a grassroots youth group in Haiti and joined a democracy movement, speaking on behalf before the 1987 elections. When the elections
were aborted, the authorities came to arrest him; for the next six months,
Mr. Alexis hid out and slept in a cave. He continued his work but covertly.
The following year, he was again threatened with arrest. After another
period in hiding, he sold his plot of land and bought passage on a boat to
Miami. When the boat was interdicted, the INS asked all the Haitians, as a
group, why they had left Haiti and if they feared being returned. Mr. Alexis
was returned.[43]

Mr. Philogéne, also a teacher, had also been active in the 1987 election
campaign and a member of the democracy movement. When he denounced
abuses by the local authorities, he, his wife, and their three children were
arrested. A public outcry led to their release, but the authorities returned to
arrest him again. Mr. Philogéne went into hiding, where he remained until,

in 1989, he sold a cow to pay for his journey to the United States. On board the ship, Mr. Philogéne was part of a group that was asked why they had left Haiti. He replied that "he had left because he did not feel safe in Haiti, and wanted to ask for asylum in the United States. The INS officer ignored him and went on to the next person. He was returned to Haiti along with the other passengers on the boat."[44]

In two respects, those who argue for interdiction are correct. The Haitians do sell their land, their livestock, their meager savings to pay for passage on treacherous boats. And certainly they come in search of a better life. But a grant of asylum does not hinge on how one paid one's passage. Nor does it preclude the impoverished. But if the refugee is a Haitian, and if he is interdicted on open waters, those two factors will probably determine that he will not be permitted to ask for asylum.

Sometimes he will not be permitted to speak at all. Mr. Dellotte and his family had gotten into a land dispute with the military. When soldiers shot his mother and killed his two uncles, Dellotte fled. He continued to oppose the government and to work for change. On September 11, 1988, he was in a church when the macoutes attacked, killing thirteen and injuring at least seventy-seven. Dellotte left Haiti by boat. The boat was interdicted, but no one on the Coast Guard ship asked his reasons for leaving Haiti. After he was returned to Haiti, however, the Haitian Red Cross met him, gave him ten dollars, and asked him where he lived and why he had fled.[45]

The Refugee Act, with its affirmation of the right to seek asylum and its guarantees against refoulement, had been enacted by the Congress in March of 1980. By September of 1981, the provisions of the act for the protection of asylum seekers had been reduced to rhetoric. The rights of asylum seekers who reached the United States could be defended, affirmed by the courts, and protected. The asylum-hearing process itself could also be reformed to assure greater fairness, and it would be. But escapees who could not reach the United States would be afforded neither protection nor fairness. Interdiction was the ultimate antidote to the Refugee Act.

In 1981, the Haitians had been effectively excluded. But now civil wars in Central America were driving other refugees northward. The Reagan Task Force on Immigration and Refugee Policy saw them not as people whose lives were in peril, but as people who imperiled the American way of life.

> Apart from the concern with overall numbers of immigrants, there is also concern over the composition of immigration. Some members of Congress and the public fear that newly arriving immigrants and refugees will not be assimilated into the national "melting pot" and that one or a few language groups, particularly the Hispanics, have come to dominate immigration.[46]

Interdiction along the southern land border would be far more difficult than interdiction of the Haitians at sea had been. But the efficacy of conventional weapons—detention and denial of due process—had been proved. These would be the government's first line of defense against the new threat of mass escape from Central America. In the year since the passage of the Refugee Act, responsibility for refugees had become returning refugees to their country of origin; "humanitarian concern" had become "humane deterrence."

1. Poster distributed by the United Nations High Commissioner for Refugees. *Credit: Foote, Cone and Belding/UNHCR.*

2. Refugees in Germany queuing for resettlement opportunities under the International Refugee Organization in 1953. *Credit: UNHCR/IRO.*

3. Southeast Asian Boat People in the South China Sea, 1979. *Credit: UNHCR/V. Leduc.*

4. Vietnamese refugees in Malaysia. *Credit: UPI/Corbis-Bettmann.*

5. Saluting the flag on Americanization Day at the Educational Alliance, 1910.
Credit: Yivo Institute for Jewish Research.

6. Southeast Asian refugee children at Fort Indiantown Gap resettlement camp, July 4,
1975. *Credit: Charles Isaacs.*

7. Main gate, Krome North INS Detention Center, Florida. *Credit: N. L. Zucker.*

8. Central Americans at the El Centro INS Detention Center, California. *Credit: © Los Angeles Times.*

9. Signature of the death squads—the *mano blanco* (white hand)—on the door of a murdered Salvadoran. *Credit: Susan Meiselas/Magnum.*

10. Refugee family in sanctuary in Weston Priory, Weston, Vermont. *Credit: The Benedictine Monks, Weston Priory, Weston, Vermont.*

11. A Haitian intercepted by the U.S. Coast Guard and detained at Guantánamo Naval Base, 1991. *Credit: AP/Wide World Photos.*

12. Cubans detained at Guantánamo Naval Base, September 13, 1994. *Credit: Omaha World-Herald/J. Beiermann.*

13. Haitian demonstrators, New York City. *Credit: Rocco Galatioto/Center for Migration Studies of New York, Inc.*

14. A drawing by a Salvadoran refugee child. *Credit: N.L. Zucker.*

15. A drawing by a Salvadoran refugee child: The emblem in the upper left stands for "our country"; the skull and crossbones just below represent a death squad. *Credit: N.L. Zucker.*

5
Erecting Fences: Escape Over Land

For American refugee policy, the decade of the 1980s began in certitude and ended in doubt. The decade began with the passage of the Refugee Act of 1980, which promised that the United States would afford welcome to the persecuted of the world. But immediately after the passage of the Refugee Act, Fidel Castro opened the port of Mariel, allowing Cubans to flee north to democracy and freedom; late in 1989, the Berlin Wall came down, allowing East Germans to flee west to democracy and freedom. On November 21, 1990, President George Bush declared, "The Cold War is over." But more than communism had died. In the intervening decade, all the foundations on which our previous refugee policy had been built—that refugees would provide an additional weapon in the war on communism, that American pressure groups would work with the government and not against it, and that the flow of refugees to the United States would be orderly—had gradually eroded and were now crumbling.

In 1980, President Jimmy Carter, a crusader for human rights, lost the election to Ronald Reagan, a staunch warrior against communism. Throughout the Reagan and Bush administrations, United States refugee policy was compelled unequivocally to serve foreign policy. The United States worked to overthrow the leftist government of Nicaragua while it lent its support to the right-wing Salvadoran and Guatemalan governments. Escapees from Nicaragua were acknowledged as refugees; escapees from El Salvador and Guatemala were dismissed as economic migrants. The government applied to the unwanted asylum seekers its established means of deterrence: detention of asylum seekers, denial of due process, even an attempt at interdiction. Religious groups and human rights advocates again sued and again won their cases, for hundreds of thousands of Central Americans. But the cause of the Central American escapees had even broader support.

Many in the American public were opposed to the administration's Central American policies; for some that opposition became support for the sanctuary movement, which defended Salvadorans and Guatemalans. The movement was soon discovered by the media, which brought sanctuary and the condition of the Central Americans into every American household. From there, the issues were brought to the Congress, where bill after bill was introduced urging that Central Americans be given temporary safe haven in the United States. The sanctuary movement evolved into much more than an expression of support for particular groups of refugees. It also came to function as a kind of shadow image of the government's refugee programs, screening Central Americans, determining the validity of their claims of persecution, and offering them resettlement assistance.

The ability of the Central American escapees to find employment came from another, and most unlikely, source—the business community. In the early eighties, the economy was growing and there was a significant need for unskilled labor, not only in agriculture but also in the service industries. By the end of the decade, however, the profligate economy of the earlier years had spent itself into debt. Domestically, restrictionists and isolationists once again promised their snake-oil panaceas: "Illegal immigrants" were stealing American jobs and bleeding American taxpayers; posing as asylum seekers, they were manipulating the immigration system and confounding the courts. The American public demanded that the gate be barred. More than at any time previously, asylum seekers were seen as illegal entrants, as opportunists, as a hole in the public purse. Public officials correctly inferred that the path to election was paved with the promise to restrict illegal immigration, to cleanse the asylum system of economic migrants.

In fact, the refugee flows from Nicaragua, El Salvador, and Guatemala, like those from Cuba and Haiti, were a result of both economic problems (in some countries an acute crisis, in others chronic deprivation) and political turmoil (repression, random violence and civil war). Although conditions differed in the five countries, it was the combination of economic and political factors that enabled the United States to respond inequitably to their refugees. Following its own dictates, the United States could choose to close one eye and look only through the other: to ignore (as it did for the Cubans and the Nicaraguans) the economic deprivation and see only the political, or (as in the case of the Haitians, Salvadorans, and Guatemalans) to ignore the political problems and look only at the economic. Anticommunist foreign policy determined which eye would be blind and which would see. But refugee flows are *never* driven by pure, uncomplicated political forces. Political instability itself creates economic insecurity.

Cecilia Menjívar has argued cogently, "If buses are burned, bridges are blown up and people cannot go to work or school, or if the political turmoil interferes with the means to earn a living, it becomes impossible to disentangle political from economic reasons for migrating."[1] Between 1989 and 1992, Menjívar interviewed and surveyed Salvadoran migrants in San Francisco. She asked the respondents to list all the reasons that they had left El Salvador and then to rank the three most important. Their answers revealed that they had left primarily for political reasons but had had economic motivations as well. "Force/fear of persecution" had impelled over 54 percent; membership in a political association, nearly 37 percent; and ideological opposition, nearly 29 percent. Yet over 44 percent cited "harsh economic conditions," and nearly 46 percent a "better future," as reasons to leave. Menjívar concluded, "Although respondents selected answers from both political and economic sets of responses, the answers were concentrated in the more extreme categories, 'force or fear of persecution' and 'harsh economic conditions.' "[2] For the Salvadoran escapees, as for many others, political forces were inextricably intertwined with economic forces.

Moreover, the frequent invocation of the "magnet effect," of the specter of floods of asylum seekers, is disingenuous. From 1980 to 1988, the United States issued over half a million immigrant visas to Mexicans.[3] The critical difference between Mexicans and Salvadorans for the United States lay in two areas: selection and foreign policy. Immigrants can be selected, asylees can not. High numbers of immigrant visas can reward cooperative governments; high numbers of asylum grants can punish the uncooperative. Every grant of asylum is an explicit criticism of conditions in the sending country. In the 1980s, the United States forbore to criticize too harshly the governments of El Salvador and Guatemala, governments that were our allies in the war against communism.

Ronald Reagan saw two worlds—communist and free. Even in the Americas, he divided the map: Central America became an area in which communist Cuba, bent on domination, had established a base, in Nicaragua, and whose next target was El Salvador. And, as Reagan repeatedly warned, "El Salvador . . . is nearer to Texas than Texas is to Massachusetts. Central America is simply too close, and the strategic stakes are too high, for us to ignore the danger of governments seizing power there with ideological and military ties to the Soviet Union."[4]

Ronald Reagan had an extraordinary ability to gauge the concerns of the average American, who was less threatened by the encroachments of communism in Central America than by the encroachments of newcomers in his or her community. The Mariel boatlift had aroused widespread fears. Reagan's administration exploited those fears in the service of its foreign policy. As Loescher and Scanlan have observed, "Rather than argue that more refugees from Cuba and other nations in the Caribbean basin provide a symbolic repudiation of Communism, Reagan policy makers . . . reversed the traditional rhetoric by implying that the spread of Communism poses a new immigration threat to the United States."[5] In June of 1983, Reagan warned that if communism was not defeated in Central America, "the result could be a tidal wave of refugees—and this time they'd be feet people, not boat people—swarming into our country seeking a safe haven from communist repression to our south."[6] The image—"feet people"—was brilliantly chosen: The refugees would descend, not just on Florida, but on our entire southern border; from there they would "swarm," like killer bees, into every area of "our country."

The image was powerful, and it was wielded like a battering ram. Secretary of State Alexander M. Haig, Jr., warned the nation's governors that if communism in Central America were not stopped, there would be a flood of refugees that "would make the Cuban influx look like child's play."[7] Secretary of State George P. Schultz, in a speech in Dallas, Texas, began by cautioning Texans that "only the stability of our neighbors will prevent unprecedented flows of refugees northward to this country."[8] So compelling was the specter of refugees that it was raised before the Organization of American States. Addressing that organization, President Reagan threatened that Cuba might succeed in its "attempt to impose a Marxist-Leninist dictatorship on the people of El Salvador as part of a larger imperialistic plan. . . ." Unless the United States took decisive action, there would be "more regimes so incompetent yet so totalitarian that their citizens' only hope [would become] that of one day migrating to other American nations, as in recent years they have come to the United States."[9] But the image was not only powerful, it was also dangerous. Representative Les AuCoin of Oregon called it "the latest version of the yellow peril argument we heard in the Fifties. Wittingly or unwittingly, it's an appeal to the darkest part of the American character."[10]

Moral objections aside, refugees were a symbol that could be manipulated by policy makers. For years, escapees from communism had been "voting with their feet"; now escapees from right-wing governments had become "feet people." Refugees do vote with their feet, not just against communism but against all forms of oppression. The rallying cry of the 1980s became *control*—control of our neighborhoods, control of our borders. The goal of American refugee policy seemed to be to turn all refugee flows into managed migrations.

Refugee admissions, unlike grants of asylum, can be managed. Reagan's attorney general William French Smith explained how this was done:

> Before the person may be granted refugee status . . . there must be two determinations made: First, whether refugee numbers have been allocated to persons in the region of the person's nationality; and second, whether the person falls into a group or category of persons "of special humanitarian concern" as determined by Congress and the President. If these factors are

not present, the person will not qualify for a grant of refugee status even if he meets the refugee definition in [the Refugee Act].[11]

Allocations are made each year to specific regions of the world. In the years 1982 to 1990, the United States admitted nearly 300,000 refugees from the Soviet Union and Eastern Europe, over 350,000 from the Near East and South Asia, and over 430,000 from East Asia. In that same period, slightly more than 21,000 refugees were admitted from Africa, nearly all of them from Marxist Ethiopia. From Latin America, the United States admitted 8,208 Cubans, 1,103 Nicaraguans, and 147 Salvadorans.[12] Allocations for Latin America in the 1980s were intended almost exclusively for Cubans; the levels rose and fell each year as a factor of US-Cuba relations. When the United States wished to pressure Cuba, it lowered the regional refugee allocation; at other times, if it was hoped that Cuba would be cooperative, the ceiling was raised.[13] (Refugee allocations, of course, were intended for Cubans who applied for refugee status from within the country. Cubans who fled directly to the United States were automatically given asylum and no limits were set on their numbers.) No explanation has been given for the low number of Nicaraguans accepted as refugees. One possible reason, however, might have been that granting refugee status to Nicaraguans would have increased the pressure on the administration to also admit Salvadorans.

Of the 147 Salvadorans admitted in this period, 93 came in one year, 1983, when, at the request of the UN High Commissioner for Refugees, the United States accepted 50 political prisoners who had been given amnesty and their families. The political prisoners were accepted as refugees only after considerable debate among members of the administration. Some officials argued that admitting the refugees would be an admission that the Salvadoran government did persecute political opponents. One official was quoted as saying, "Many conservatives were dead set against taking any. They said this would leave the impression that there are refugees from El Salvador and that El Salvador does not protect its people."[14]

With the gate of refugee admission virtually closed to Salvadoran escapees, the only legal avenue remaining to them was to enter the United States without entry documents and to apply for political asylum. But this gate of entry opened no more easily than the other. The Immigration Service was ill prepared to decide asylum claims. The service almost always granted asylum to applicants from unfriendly, or communist countries, and denied asylum to applicants from friendly, or right-wing countries. From June of 1983 to March of 1991, 2.8 percent of Salvadoran applicants were given asylum. In that same period, approval rates were 74.5 percent for Soviet citizens, 69 percent for Chinese, and 61 percent for Iranians.[15]

The Salvadorans were by far the largest population of Central Americans to seek refuge in the United States. The Reagan and Bush administrations argued that the Salvadorans were simply following a long-established stream of migrant workers from El Salvador. Yet there is no evidence that Salvadorans had migrated to the United States in large numbers earlier than 1980, when government attacks on civilians began.[16] A sudden increase in the number of Salvadorans being apprehended by the INS occurred in 1980; this was followed by similar surges in 1981, 1983, and 1984.

A study was conducted by William Stanley, of the Massachusetts Institute of Technology, to analyze why the Salvadorans migrated to the United States.[17] Stanley wanted to learn whether there was any correlation between the level of political violence in El Salvador and the number of Salvadorans coming to the United States. He found that when political murders declined in El Salvador, so did the number of Salvadorans apprehended by the INS; conversely, when military sweeps were broadened, or when the death squads heightened their campaigns of terror, the number of INS apprehensions "climbed dramatically."[18] Stanley recognized that, as a measure, apprehensions could simply reflect greater enforcement efforts along the border. He controlled for this factor by including in his data Mexican apprehensions, as well as Salvadoran. He also tracked economic factors that might have pushed Salvadorans to emigrate. All of his research led him to conclude that "fear of political violence is an important and probably the dominant motivation of Salvadorans who have migrated to the United States since the beginning of 1979. The level of political violence in El Salvador is closely associated with the numbers of Salvadorans."[19]

The counterpart to Stanley's study was carried out by Segundo Montes, of Central American University in El Salvador. Montes studied the areas from which the émigrés had come and found that the provinces with the highest levels of political conflict sent the largest proportions of their populations to the United States.[20] Finally, a study comparing Mexicans and Central Americans in the United States found, "While Mexican migration is, and has been for most of this century, essentially a labor migration, a large proportion of . . . Central American[s] migrated for political reasons."[21] None of the Mexicans surveyed reported political motives for their migration, whereas over 40 percent of the Central American men and nearly 38 percent of the Central American women did. The predominant reason given was to escape from political conflicts and civil war.[22]

Whatever people's reasons might have been for fleeing their country, those reasons were obscured by the shadow of great numbers. During the 1980s, the asylum system was inundated with applications, largely from Central America. From 1984 to 1990, the system adjudicated 48,000 Nicaraguan claims, 45,000 Salvadoran, and 9,500 Guatemalan. Of those, 26 percent of the Nicaraguan claims were approved, but only 2.6 percent of the Salvadoran and 1.8 percent of the Guatemalan claims were approved.[23] The accusation was often made that Salvadoran and Guatemalan asylum seekers fell victim to a foreign policy bias in the State and Justice departments. The Reagan administration countered that charge with the claim that only slightly more than one-quarter of Nicaraguan asylum claims were approved, but it neglected to point out that even this rate was ten times the rate for Salvadorans.

For most of the 1980s, the INS asylum officers and immigration judges were poorly prepared for their jobs. Fewer than 2 percent of INS officers had had any training at all in asylum issues, and that 2 percent received fewer than three hours of such instruction.[24] The officers themselves freely acknowledged their ignorance. One examiner justified his asylum decisions this way: "We can't make a decision solely from the evidence presented because most people can't meet the strict standards. . . . I never ask a person anything. I just look and see if the person belongs to a nationality group that everyone agrees are refugees like the Poles."[25] The director of the INS detention center in El Centro, California, was less circumspect; he asserted that the Salvadorans were "just peasants who are coming to the United States for a welfare card and a Cadillac."[26]

A few Salvadorans appealed their decisions. But the immigration judges, though somewhat better informed, adhered almost slavishly to the administration's foreign policy, ignoring any evidence of persecution by the Salvadoran government. A twenty-nine-year-old Salvadoran, for example, claimed that "because he had participated in the Salvadoran teachers' union, he had been arrested and tortured with acid, and a brother had been kidnapped, tortured and decapitated." Doctors from Amnesty International corroborated his story, and the INS did not deny it. The immigration judge denied him asylum, however, explaining:

> The applicant has described the suffering which he and other family members had unfortunately endured during the civil strife in El Salvador, suffering which has been similarly experienced by other groups and political factions operation [sic] in El Salvador. The problems of the applicant and his family members, however, do not stem from persecution but from the civil strife which has torn El Salvador apart over the past five to nine years. The tragedy of El Salvador is that the suffering, the armed kidnapping and other excesses are not confined to one particular group but are endured and perpetrated by all. For these reasons, the applicant has failed to establish that he qualifies as a refugee.[27]

The judge had conveniently confused two separate causes for refugee flight: fear of persecution and civil strife. While civil strife is not a basis for a grant of asylum, fear of persecution is. The Salvadoran man had shown, with reliable corroboration, that he had a well-founded fear of persecution. He had been targeted by agents of the government, yet the judge ignored this claim and averred that he was a victim only of civil war.

Asylum would be denied to Salvadorans even when they claimed to have been persecuted by opponents of the government, the guerrillas. A twenty-seven-year-old woman said that, because she taught in a government school, she, as well as other teachers, had received death threats written by the guerrillas. Her petition was denied by the immigration judge, who stated, "These threats were general in nature . . . and part of the pattern of guerrilla warfare in the ongoing civil war occurring in El Salvador since 1978 or 1979."[28]

A comprehensive study of the asylum system, conducted by Deborah Anker, a lecturer on law at Harvard University, concluded that the asylum system was based on "ad hoc rules and standards." The study found that decisions were influenced by "ideological preferences and unreasoned and uninvestigated political judgments."[29]

Both INS officers and immigration judges relied heavily on the advisory opinions of the State Department's Bureau of Human Rights and Humanitarian Affairs (BHRHA). These opinions mirrored quite precisely the foreign and military policies of the administration. An internal study by the Immigration Service reported:

> Certain nationalities appear to benefit from presumptive status while others do not.
> For example, for an El Salvadoran national to receive a favorable asylum advisory opinion, he or she must have a "classic textbook case." On the other hand, BHRHA sometimes recommends favorable action where the applicant cannot meet the individual well-founded fear of persecution test. This happened in December 1981 a week after martial law was declared in Poland. Seven Polish crewmen jumped ship and applied for asylum in Alaska. Even before seeing the asylum applications, a State Department official said, "We're going to approve them." All the applications, in the view of INS senior officials, were extremely weak. In one instance, the crewman said the reason he feared returning to Poland was that he had once attended a Solidarity rally (he was one of the more than 100,000 participants at the rally). The crewman had never been a member of Solidarity, never participated in any political activity, etc. His claim was approved within forty-eight hours.[30]

A General Accounting Office study found that this foreign policy bias pervaded asylum decisions even when the applicant had been subjected to torture. Torture victims from El Salvador had an approval rate of 4 percent, from Nicaragua 15 percent, from Iran 64 percent, and from Poland 80 percent.[31]

But Salvadorans confronted a wall far more impenetrable than an inept bureaucracy and doctrinaire policy makers. That wall was the refugee law itself and the definition on which it is based. While a number of Central Americans did fear persecution, many others feared civil war, with its attendant dangers. Dr. Edelberto Torres-Rivas, a Guatemalan scholar, has described their plight:

> Central American refugees often are not persecuted for reasons of religion, race, or political opinion. Generally speaking, the problem is not one of convictions *per se,* rather something much more basic and thus much more tragic: having to save one's life without even knowing why it is endangered.[32]

Refugee law did not address their condition. Government policy makers chose to ignore it. Only a small group of private citizens, acting outside of the legal system, responded. In July of 1980, while Cubans and Haitians were paying for small boats to carry them over the water to South Florida, Central Americans were paying *coyotes,* smugglers of undocumented entrants, to carry them over the desert to the southwestern states. One coyote, having collected his fees from twenty-six Salvadorans, abandoned them without water in the Arizona desert, just outside of Tucson. Half of the Salvadorans died; the others survived by drinking aftershave, deodorant, even their own urine.[33] Church members in the area assisted the survivors but were horrified by the stories they told. When the Salvadorans were arrested, Tucson churches raised money to pay for their bond and for legal assistance so that they could plead their cases for asylum.

The INS fell back on its established practices, curtailing the rights of detained asylum seekers to due process, including the right to speak with a legal representative. One of those legal representatives was Jim Corbett, a rancher with a graduate degree in philosophy from Harvard, tough, contentious, and moral. While Corbett was at the Nogales jail, interviewing a Salvadoran, he learned of other Salvadorans in detention who also needed representation. Corbett left the jail to obtain the G-28 forms that they could sign, naming him their legal representative. When he returned, he was told that all the Salvadorans had been moved; the INS refused to disclose where they had been moved to.[34] Similarly, at a detention center in Southern California, the INS was keeping paralegals from their clients. When Corbett visited Mexican jails, he found Salvadorans with strong claims who, when they had approached the US border and tried to ask for political asylum, had been turned over to the Mexican authorities to be returned to El Salvador.[35]

Corbett needed help and turned to John Fife, pastor of Southside Presbyterian Church in Tucson. Fife's congregation was soon joined by other religious bodies—in California; Washington, D.C.; Ohio; and New York—which formed a network to offer to Central American refugees sanctuary, legal assistance, and support, and to lobby Washington for a halt to the deportations. By March of 1987, the number of declared sanctuaries around the country had grown to 379. Most of these declarations were by congregations, universities, and community groups; there were also 22 city councils, 28 national bodies (many of those religious), and two states, New Mexico and New York.[36] Nine months later, the number had grown to 448 sanctuary locations.

The sanctuary movement became an underground adaptation of a legal refugee program. The Central Americans passed through an initial screening, then through processes that strongly resembled "admission," "reception," and eventually "resettlement." The first step in the sanctuary process was to determine which escapees had credible claims. Nearly all those accepted into sanctuary were able to offer actual proof of imprisonment or torture. Jim Corbett told of a Salvadoran man who had been imprisoned in San Salvador, where he had been tortured with electrodes placed in his ears, damaging his eardrums. A woman was tortured and raped; some of her children were killed. Both had documents to support their claims. Guatemalans and Nicaraguans, as well as Salvadorans, entered the United States with the help of sanctuary workers.

While officially recognized refugees were often flown to refugee processing centers and then to the United States, refugees in sanctuary traveled to a series of safe houses. They were met in the United States, not at a port of entry by an INS official, but in the desert by a sanctuary worker. Within the country, refugees in sanctuary were "resettled" by congregations, which supported them. As for all refugees, the goal was self-sufficiency, but in sanctuary, this often meant easing the refugee into the underground community.

But the movement also left an important and lasting legacy to the legal system. Sanctuary exposed the biases and the inadequacies of the asylum system. As a result, national organizations such as the National Lawyers Guild and the American Civil Liberties Union became involved. The guild established a project to train lawyers to represent Central American asylum applicants. The ACLU created a computerized file of some 30,000 individuals who had been victims of human rights abuses in El Salvador alone.[37]

Salvadorans who fled to the United States often found themselves victims of human rights abuses here as well. Crosby Wilfredo Orantes-Hernandez crossed the border into the United States illegally, late in 1981. INS agents apprehended him as he was getting off a bus in Culver City, California; they struck him in the nose and mouth with their pistols.

Bleeding severely, Orantes-Hernandez was taken to a detention center. There the immigration agents goaded him to sign a voluntary departure form. They did not inform him of his rights: to a formal hearing, to counsel, and to ask for asylum.[38] But Orantes-Hernandez would not be one of the thousands quickly deported and as quickly forgotten. He became the named plaintiff in a class action suit, *Orantes-Hernandez v. Meese and INS,* which asserted that the Immigration Service coerced Salvadorans into signing voluntary departure agreements.[39]

In 1982, the district court in California found that:

> The evidence presented by Plaintiffs shows that Salvadorans are frequently arrested, deposited in waiting rooms, interrogated, put onto buses, and flown back to El Salvador all in a matter of hours. Often the aliens do not understand the language in which they are addressed, much less the chain of events which has been set in motion. In this environment, "coercion" is not limited to physical force or outright threats. The courts on numerous occasions have recognized that the more subtle effects of atmosphere, setting, and the omission of certain statements of advisals may have an equally coercive effect. *See, e.g., Miranda v. Arizona,* 384 US 436, 448 (1966) ("Coercion can be mental as well as physical, and the blood of the accused is not the only hallmark of an unconstitutional inquisition").[40]

In the California courtroom, much more than the plaintiffs' rights was at risk. For some, it was also their lives. Witnesses testified that El Salvador lacked a functioning judicial system, and that Salvadoran officials and members of the security forces were not prosecuted for the torture, killings, and disappearances of Salvadorans. Nor was there any government investigation in El Salvador into human rights abuses. Perhaps even more chilling was the testimony that the US State Department withheld from the plaintiffs documentation of these abuses.[41] The court, taking judicial notice of conditions in El Salvador, found that the Salvadorans faced "irreparable injury" if they were to be deported.

The district court issued a preliminary injunction against the INS, enjoining them from pressuring Salvadorans to sign voluntary departure forms, either through "threats, misrepresentation, subterfuge or other forms of coercion. . . . " The INS was also required to read to the detainees, in both Spanish and English, a notice of their rights, including the right to be represented by an attorney, to a deportation hearing, and to apply for political asylum, as well as the right to request voluntary departure.[42]

While advocates battled on behalf of the Salvadorans in a California courtroom, the sanctuary movement pressured the Congress. They persuaded Senator Dennis DeConcini of Arizona, along with Congressman Joseph Moakley in the House, to introduce in 1983 a bill to temporarily suspend the deportation of Salvadorans in the United States. Senator DeConcini was not proposing a new idea. The suspension of deportation was known at that time as extended voluntary departure (EVD) and differed from both refugee status and asylum.

Sometimes individuals from a particular country were in the United States when conditions in their own country changed—there might have been a revolution, a civil war, or a government crackdown on dissidents—and it became unsafe for them to return. In such cases, citizens of that country might have been granted extended voluntary departure. The group's departure from the United States was not "voluntary" but it was deferred, or "extended," until it was considered safe for them to return home. EVD did not require that the members of the group fear persecution. EVD was awarded because of general conditions, not because of the individual's own condition.

EVD had previously been awarded to a number of national groups. Nicaraguans had received EVD because of "unsettled conditions in Nicaragua" and "unstable conditions currently existing there." Poles were granted the status because of "continued denial of rights to the Polish people . . . " and because of "unstable conditions currently existing in the country." Lebanese could stay in the United States because "civil strife in the country continues." The departure date for Ethiopians was extended because of "circumstances currently prevailing there" and "unsettled conditions."[43] Although often vague about conditions in a country of origin, the INS could be quite specific in *not* requiring that citizens of that country present a well-founded fear of persecution. For example, the service ordered that Afghanis "who do not apply for asylum but resist returning to Afghanistan because of the turmoil prevailing in that country rather than because of a fear of persecution should be granted extended voluntary departure and work authorization in increments of one year."[44]

If EVD did not demand that the members of the group fear persecution if they returned, it also did not require that they had feared persecution before they left. (Such a fear would have made them eligible to apply for refugee status or asylum.) In fact, those who were given EVD had usually come to the United States for ordinary reasons—to vacation, for example, or to study or work. It was only after they were in this country that conditions in their own country changed, making their return inadvisable.

The State Department actively opposed the DeConcini-Moakley bill. The department insisted that Salvadorans had first come to the United States to seek work. Further, they had available to them the avenue of legal immigration from El Salvador. Finally, if they feared persecution, they should apply for asylum. Assistant Secretary William L. Ball III summarized the arguments: "*We oppose EVD for Salvadorans.* Normal immigration, coupled with asylum for true refugees, is adequate to allow a controlled flow of immigrants into the US and to meet legitimate humanitarian concerns (italics in original)."[45] None of these reasons, of course, had been invoked when EVD had been awarded to other groups.

In plain fact, the administration had two reasons for not granting EVD to the Salvadorans. The first reason was fear of numbers. Like many others, Elliot Abrams, assistant secretary of state for human rights and humanitarian affairs, feared what he called the magnet effect. Secretary Abrams explained:

> If you look at the four countries for which there is EVD today, one thing in common about them is they are far away, and that is not a coincidence. That is, we are extremely reluctant to grant EVD to any country which is nearby and has had a long history of massive illegal immigration to the United States for economic reasons.[46]

The second reason was foreign policy. A regional commissioner of the INS stated the point directly; he wrote, "Extended Voluntary Departure is a foreign relations tool."[47]

During the Reagan and Bush administrations, not only extended voluntary departure, but the escapees it would have protected became a "foreign policy tool." In April of 1987, Salvadoran President José Napoléon Duarte appealed to President Reagan to allow Salvadorans to remain in the United States. President Duarte argued that the remittances sent home by Salvadorans in the United States were necessary to help rebuild the Salvadoran economy. In an ironic reversal, the request was supported by Secretary of State George Schultz and by Assistant Secretary Elliot Abrams. Abrams had volubly opposed protecting Salvadorans, but he now advocated protecting the Salvadoran government. This was an entirely new interpretation of the arguments over whether the escapees were "economic" or "political" migrants.

In a letter to the *New York Times,* President Duarte publicly pressed his case. "Why should an opponent of democracy in El Salvador, a knowing or unknowing supporter of Marxist terrorists, be granted permanent political asylum, while the son who sends three-fourths of his income to his mother in a small Salvadoran village is denied even temporary reprieve?"[48] Despite Duarte's arguments, which should have appealed to both Cold Warriors and supporters of motherhood, the White House turned down the request. President Duarte's arguments might well have lost him his case. It was later reported that officials in the State Department agreed that Salvadorans in the United States were sympathizers with the Marxist guerrillas attempting to overthrow the government.[49] Whether for individual grants of asylum or for blanket grants of temporary protection, the deciding factor remained Cold War prejudices.

The influence of foreign policy on refugee admissions and asylum decisions grew to be more than a bias; under Reagan, foreign policy became virtually a directive. In 1986, it was learned that the Justice Department was drafting new procedures under which it was stated, "Polish nationals who are unwilling to return to Poland due to conditions there and who request or have requested political asylum or refugee status are presumed to be refugees within the meaning" of the Refugee Act. Attorney General Edwin Meese felt the directive reflected a policy he wanted to establish for citizens of communist countries. Another official explained, "We take tremendous heat from conservatives because our asylum policy is inconsistent with our foreign policy."[50] Shortly thereafter, the district director for the INS in Florida announced that he would no longer deport Nicaraguans because, he felt, he "would personally—not just as a government official, but personally—have trouble sending people from a Communist country back to that country." He added that by law he had "the authority and discretion" to make such a decision.[51]

Attorney General Meese used his authority to extend that policy nationally; on July 8, 1987, he directed the INS to take special actions toward Nicaraguans in the United States. The Immigration Service, was, first, not to deport any Nicaraguan with a well-founded fear of persecution. Beyond not deporting Nicaraguans, the service was to actively assist them: Not only would all Nicaraguans who asked for work authorization be "entitled" to receive it, but the INS was "directed to encourage and expedite" their applications. Most important, INS officials were ordered to "encourage Nicaraguans whose claims for asylum or withholding of deportation have been denied to reapply for reopening or rehearing" of their claims.[52] The previous year, the asylum approval rate for Nicaraguans had been 27 percent. In 1987, it leaped to 82 percent, higher than for any other nationality.[53]

In Washington, the attorney general had ordered preferential treatment for Nicaraguans. In California, the district court now ordered equal treatment for Salvadorans. Six years after Judge David V. Kenyon had first issued his preliminary injunction against the attorney general and the INS, in April of 1988, the class action suit of *Orantes-Hernandez* was decided.[54] The judge ruled on behalf of the Salvadorans and against the attorney general and found the INS still to be in violation of his order that Salvadorans be informed of their rights. He ordered that:

Defendants shall not employ threats, misrepresentation, subterfuge or other forms of coercion, or in any other way attempt to persuade or dissuade class members when informing them of the availability of voluntary departure. . . .

Among the acts prohibited to the INS were:

Misrepresenting the meaning of political asylum and giving improper and incomplete legal advice to detained class members;
Telling class members that if they apply for asylum they will remain in detention for a long period of time, without mentioning the possibility of release on bond . . . ;
Telling class members that their asylum applications will be denied, that Salvadorans do not get asylum . . . ;
Representing to class members that the information on the asylum application will be sent to El Salvador;
Refusing to allow class members to contact an attorney. . . . [55]

A similar suit had been brought in Texas by Salvadorans together with Guatemalans. The Texas court joined in the *Orantes-Hernandez* ruling, effectively preventing the INS from continuing to coerce Central Americans. The court's ruling placed the ability to request asylum alongside the most cherished American rights:

This Court fully appreciates the burden that may result to defendants due to the requirements of this Order. Providing refuge to those facing persecution in their homeland, however, goes to the very heart of the principles and moral precepts upon which this country and its Constitution were founded. It is unavoidable that some burdens result from the protection of these principles. To let these same principles go unprotected would amount to nothing less than a sacrilege.[56]

But Washington had more pragmatic concerns than protecting the Constitution. The number of applications for asylum and for work authorization had soared. INS Commissioner Alan C. Nelson complained of "an unprecedented increase in asylum requests" in FY 1988, more than two and a half times the number there had been in FY 1987. The increase, he believed, was not the result of increased persecution in the applicants' home countries; rather, it was due to "the change from a discretionary grant . . . to a mandatory grant of employment authorization. . . . "[57]

From May 30 through December 8, 1988, Harlingen, Texas, had received over 27,000 applications for a grant of asylum. Approximately half of those applications came from Nicaraguans, one-quarter from Salvadorans, and an eighth each from Guatemalans and Hondurans. Miami,

Florida, was receiving 1,000 applications a week; the Miami district now had a backlog of 50,000 applications, of which 35,000 were from Nicaraguans.[58] On December 2, Acting Associate Attorney General Francis A. Keating II wrote that he was "deeply concerned by recent reports that large numbers of Central American nationals, primarily Nicaraguans, are streaming across the Border near Harlingen. State and local officials believe the situation there is out of control." He urged that the Nicaraguan Review Program be rescinded.[59]

Attorney General Meese, a staunch supporter of the Nicaraguan contras, had determined to open the outer gate wide for escaping Nicaraguans. The INS felt besieged by the resultant crush of asylum seekers; when Meese was replaced as attorney general by Dick Thornburgh, the service ran to shut an inner gate. Trapped inside were thousands of Central American refugees. Salvadorans and Guatemalans who asked asylum had always been treated inequitably; now they would be treated inhumanely.

Prior to the new directives, Central Americans who applied for asylum in South Texas had been permitted to travel onward and to have their claims adjudicated in other locations. The refugees had usually left South Texas and traveled to areas where they had family and friends to house and help them and where there was legal representation to provide evidence for their claims. But under the new INS policy, asylum applicants were confined to the Harlingen area; they were not put into detention, but were, however, left without food, shelter, or hope of employment. An INS patrol agent described what he saw:

> We were detaining no one. One hundred percent of the OTMs [Other than Mexicans] were being put on the street. It was depressing to be a law enforcement agent, to see the results of our work walk out the front door. How do we know we weren't releasing criminal elements? It was an unhealthy situation for this country. People were camped in vacant lots and in an abandoned, fenced-off motel. I wasn't proud of what we were doing."[60]

Once again, an ill-planned policy resulted in a reaction. Advocates brought suit in district court, and Judge Filemon Vela issued a temporary restraining order. The Central Americans were now free to file their applications in South Texas, then move elsewhere for adjudication. Constraint was succeeded by chaos. As thousands of Central Americans rushed to submit applications, the asylum system careened out of control. The situation has been graphically described:

> The way asylum applications were being filed had the appearance of a feeding frenzy. At the time, there was no control over frivolous applications, and

the system clearly was open to abuse. Many of the applications filed at that time were inaccurate or lacking in information upon which an asylum claim could be based; some were even identical, filled out by unscrupulous middlemen. Taxi drivers taking people to the INS office frequently filled out the asylum application forms.

The Central Americans themselves often had no idea that they were applying for asylum. They often thought the I-589s simply represented "permiso" to work and travel. It is likely that among those who filed bad applications were genuine refugees who were not aware of what they were doing and who were never asked questions relating to potential refugee status.[61]

In Miami, officials anticipated a deluge of Nicaraguans. The *Miami Herald* foretold a "tidal wave that would engulf Greater Miami, causing social and economic destruction more severe than any American city anywhere has ever experienced."[62]

On February 20, Judge Vela lifted his restraining order. On that same day, Commissioner Nelson announced a new and decisive plan for dealing with asylum claims. The new policy could be summed up in three words: deter, detain, deport. To deter future refugees, information was to be collected from asylum seekers about where they had come from, why they had left, and the routes they had followed; this information was to be shared with the CIA and the State and Defense departments. All asylum applicants in Harlingen would be detained; since there were not enough facilities to house them, tent camps were set up. The goal was to deport them as quickly as possible: asylum requests were to be processed in a single day; toward that goal, hearings were held for twenty or more Central Americans at one time. In clear violation of the *Orantes-Hernandez* ruling, the Central Americans were deprived of legal counsel and any understanding of the proceedings.[63]

One such hearing was observed by the US Committee for Refugees:

> Crammed into a small cinder-block room, the detainees in their bright orange prison uniforms watched as the [immigration] judge, in black robes, leafed through files and spoke into a tape recorder. None of the detainees was represented by legal counsel. The judge asked, "If it is necessary for me to order you deported, to which country would you wish to be sent?" Each person stood as his name was called and named his country. The judge asked each, "Is there any reason why you cannot be returned to . . . ," and then he again sorted through files trying to match the name of the country with the name of the individual. Each answered, "No."
>
> After explaining the option of voluntary departure, the judge asked, "Is the reason you do not apply because you do not have enough money to return home?" Each person answered, "Yes."
>
> The judge then ordered them all deported. He told them that they had the right to appeal to a higher court if they thought his decision was unjust. "Do

you all waive your right to appeal?" he asked. One man said, "I don't understand." The judge repeated that "you have the right to appeal to a higher court." The man fell silent as the group in unison waived their right to appeal.[64]

Later, the judge explained why he had not told the detainees that they had the right to apply for asylum. Because each person had given his home country as the country to which he wished to be sent if deported, this proved that none of them had a fear of persecution.[65] The judge failed to take into account that some of them might have been in fear of interrogation. During the *Orantes-Hernandez* trial, Dr. Saul Nieford, a clinical psychiatrist and authority on Central America was called as an expert witness. Dr. Nieford testified that Central Americans often will not reveal what has happened to them. Salvadorans, he said, suffer what he termed "frozen shame" at having survived when others did not and then having fled.[66]

The immigration judge, like the INS itself, had also ignored a basic provision of the *Orantes-Hernandez* ruling, that asylum seekers were entitled to legal counsel. On May 1, 1989, Judge David Kenyon again issued an injunction, requiring the Immigration Service to advise Salvadorans of their rights.[67] The following year, the Ninth Circuit upheld the injunction, enumerating instances of coercion by the INS. One Border Patrol agent refused to offer an asylum form, even if the alien said he feared persecution, except if the individual used the words, "I want political asylum." Another claimed never to have seen an asylum application. Another agent, when a woman refused to sign a deportation order, grabbed her hand and forced her to sign an X.[68] The government decided not to bring the case to the Supreme Court.

The INS saw itself as an enforcer of the law but not the law as it had been interpreted by the courts. The law enforced at the border could be reduced to a simple syllogism: No one could enter the United States without proper documentation; asylum seekers were undocumented; therefore, asylum seekers ought not to be permitted to enter. In fairness to the Immigration Service, it was being asked to serve two masters, and only one was the paymaster. While the courts were concerned with protecting the Constitution, Congress, responding to the voters, demanded control of the border.

Whatever victories the Central Americans might have won in American courts were hollow if they never reached the United States. The INS had devised an auxiliary plan to interdict the Central Americans and prevent them from crossing the southern border. A detailed plan of action urged that the State Department and INS "liaison . . . secure the assistance of Mexico and Central American countries to slow down the flow of illegal aliens into the United States.[69] The plan was, on its face, innocuous—to deter illegal entrants—but for the fact that, to the INS, asylum seekers from Central America were all illegal entrants. The right to request asylum was an impediment to border control, one that could, ideally, be circumvented if the Central Americans were interdicted before they could enter the asylum process.

Operation Hold the Line was put into effect in February of 1989. By June, an INS newsletter was reporting "cooperation with the Government of Mexico to stem the flow of Central American migrants through that country, including the establishment of checkpoints along transit corridors and the deportation of intercepted Central Americans."[70] One measure of the success of the initiative was that in 1990, the number of Central Americans arrested while crossing into the United States dropped by over 20 percent. For the same period, apprehensions of Mexicans increased by 26 percent.[71] As William Stanley indicated in his study, the Mexican numbers can be used as a control for economic factors. If the numbers of Central Americans had decreased because the United States was imposing stricter sanctions on the employment of illegal entrants, then the numbers of Mexicans (who migrate almost exclusively for economic reasons) would have decreased as well.

Nearly ten years after the passage of the Refugee Act, its provisions for the granting of asylum seemed utterly distorted. A comprehensive case study of the asylum system by Deborah Anker of the Harvard Law School found that "the current adjudicatory system remains one of ad hoc rules and standards. Despite Congress' goals in creating statutory asylum procedures, factors rejected by Congress—including ideological preferences and unreasoned and uninvestigated political judgments—continue to influence the decision making process."[72] Criticism of the asylum system had come from lawyers, from scholars, and from public officials. But, significantly, criticism had also come from within the government. Asylum had become a tangled knot of biases and intransigence and perseverance, of injustice and suits to win justice, of growing numbers and lessening patience, of action leading to stasis. The knot could no longer be untangled; there was no choice but to cut away the past and begin afresh.

In a few months at the end of 1990, the knot was cut and a fresh start made. The goals of the sanctuary movement had finally been achieved: Salvadorans, as a class, were given the safe haven status they had asked for. Individuals who wanted asylum were to have their cases reopened. The INS was establishing an independent asylum board. And the government had agreed not to impose its foreign policy on asylum decisions.

After nearly ten years, the DeConcini-Moakley bills to grant extended voluntary departure to Salvadorans became law. Congress had passed the landmark Immigration Act of 1990, among the provisions of which was one that Salvadorans who had been present in the United States before September 19, 1990, would be protected from deportation for a period of eighteen months, until June of 1992. The specific cutoff date was inserted so that there would be no magnet effect, no incentive for Salvadorans to continue to migrate to the United States. This new status was given a new name, temporary protected status, or TPS. The attorney general was also given the power to grant TPS, at his or her discretion, to nationals fleeing armed conflict, natural disaster, or other extraordinary conditions. When the act was signed, at the end of November 1990, the INS announced that it would release all eligible Salvadorans from detention.

By 1992, the government of El Salvador and the opposing guerrilla forces had reached an agreement to end the fighting and negotiate a peace accord. There seemed to be no real obstacle to terminating the Salvadoran TPS when it was scheduled to expire in June. Salvadoran President Alfredo Cristiani wrote to President George Bush, however, asking that the temporary protected status be extended. He feared, in an echo of the Duarte appeal, that the reintegration of many Salvadorans would be too burdensome for a country that needed to rebuild itself after so many years of civil war. President Bush agreed but decided to call the extended status deferred enforced departure, or DED. The change of name—from temporary protected status to deferred enforced departure—was probably more than semantic; the new name conveyed a resolve to deport rather than a commitment to protect.

President Bill Clinton, in 1992, extended the DED status another eighteen months, until December of 1994. But future extensions were not likely. The country's restrictionist grumblings had become a strident chorus. California voters had just passed Proposition 187 to bar illegal entrants from schools, routine health care, and some social services; politicians across the country were leaping onto the bandwagon. In Washington, government officials wanted to show that temporary protection need not become permanent residency, that refugee programs could be terminated when the need for them had passed.

The granting of temporary protection to the Salvadorans was significant, but of far greater significance was the effort by the Immigration Service to reform the entire asylum adjudication system. After years of criticism by legal experts, scholars, human rights organizations, and refugee advocates, after repeated court judgments against it, the Justice Department had acquiesced in the need for reform. Acquiescence had not come easily. Since the passage of the Refugee Act in 1980, asylum claims had been adjudicated within the Immigration Service, by district directors or administrative law judges in the Executive Office of Immigration Review. Many studies of the asylum process, including studies by the INS itself, had recommended the establishment of an independent and objective body of officers trained in refugee law.[73]

Ironically, the class action suits brought by Haitians and Central Americans, which repeatedly brought judgments against the INS, may have been instrumental in the service's unwillingness to effect reform. Doris Meissner, who became the INS commissioner under Clinton, observed that the INS, under attack in the courts, could not allow itself to acknowledge its own deficiencies or any need to improve its procedures.[74] Both inside and outside the courtroom, the INS was conducting what Orwell called "the defense of the indefensible."

In 1987, the Justice Department had proposed a final asylum rule, but it had not quieted the opposition. The rule would have established the asylum corps within the INS, but it also ordered that the State Department country reports "shall be the principal source of . . . information" on country conditions.[75] A tug of war ensued between those outside the INS who wanted an unbiased, professional corps and those within it who wanted to maintain control of asylum decisions. On one side were those who saw asylum decisions as a matter of equity; on the other side were those who saw them as a matter of enforcement.

The advocates of equity won. Gene McNary became INS commissioner and in 1991 the Bush administration mandated a new corps of asylum officers, under the direction of the INS assistant commissioner for refugees, asylum and parole. The corps of asylum officers who are now in place have received instruction in human rights and refugee law and in asylum policy. They are trained in interviewing techniques and taught to be sensitive to the particular needs of refugees. A Resource Information Center has been set up to provide asylum officers with information on the countries from which the applicants come, on legal rulings, and on refugee policy.

The asylum program now has established two goals: to approve asylum claims with merit expeditiously, and to deny, just as expeditiously, claims that lack merit. Most important, the asylum interview is designed to be nonadversarial.[76] How well have these goals been achieved? One way to measure this achievement is to compare the asylum cases decided by district directors under the old system with the cases decided by the new asylum officers. In the first year, FY 1992, the percentage of cases approved overall rose from 23.6 percent to 36.8 percent. The approval rate for Salvadorans increased dramatically, from 2.8 percent to 28 percent, while that for Guatemalans rose from 2 percent to 21.1 percent. The increase in Haitian cases was still more dramatic, from 1.8 percent to 30.6 percent.[77]

By 1995, the overall number of asylum claims had dropped dramatically to less than half the number filed in 1994.[78] Two related reforms led to this outcome: First, the INS ruled that work permits would be given only to those individuals who were granted asylum or whose cases had not been decided within 180 days; second, the great majority of cases were decided within 60 days. The two factors together discouraged the filing of frivolous claims and benefited genuine asylum seekers. A major examination by the National Asylum Study Project of Harvard Law School of decisions by the asylum officer corps "found that overall it is a substantially more professional, informed, and impartial body of asylum decision-makers than the INS examiners who adjudicated asylum claims previously."[79] Many suggestions have been offered to further improve their work, but it is clear that the new system can function fairly and effectively.

With Salvadorans already in the United States given temporary protection, and with asylum decisions about to be vested in an autonomous body, the Justice Department agreed, in late 1990, to settle a five-year-old class action suit, *American Baptist Churches v. Thornburgh,* known by its initials as the *ABC* case. The suit had been brought originally on behalf of sanctuary workers, who argued that the protection of Central Americans was their right under the First Amendment's guarantee of the "free exercise of religion." It had been transformed into a class action suit that charged that the government had not adjudicated neutrally and nonpolitically, as the law requires, the asylum applications of Salvadorans and Guatemalans. The government agreed to reopen the Salvadoran and Guatemalan asylum cases. In the agreement, the government specified that, in considering these cases, it would *not* give weight to border control, to American foreign policy, or to whether the applicant came from a country allied politically with the United States.

Under the agreement, class members could not be deported or detained while their asylum claims were being adjudicated. They were, however, entitled to employment authorizations. Central American asylum cases would be heard by the newly established asylum officers corps, which, though within the INS, was autonomous. For the government, however, a new problem presented itself. The class of asylum cases included those Salvadorans who had registered for temporary protected status in 1991. Knowing of the government bias against them, and fearing almost certain deportation, many had not previously asked for asylum. As many as 235,000 *ABC* class members may in the future file asylum claims.[80] Rather than burden the asylum corps with this nearly insurmountable backlog, some observers have suggested that the class members be granted permanent resident status.

Critics cite this backlog as evidence that the asylum system is "out of control," a legal escape clause for illegal entrants; they argue that applying for asylum ought to be made more difficult. In fact, the backlog grew not because it was too easy to ask for asylum, but because, for a whole class of applicants, it was too difficult. Had the government applied the law fairly and evenhandedly, there would have been no class action suits and no adverse rulings, and, finally, the backlogs would have been far smaller.

The government had fought the Central American asylum seekers on many fronts. It had fought at the borders, in the bureaucracy, in the Congress, and in the courts. It had lost on several of these fronts. The borders remained permeable; the bureaucracy had acceded to reform. Congress had granted the Salvadorans temporary protected status, and the courts had affirmed their right to due process of law. If the government had lost some battles, however, it was determined not to lose the war. The front now shifted east, as once again Haitians and then Cubans began arriving in large numbers. This time the government would take preemptive action. It was determined to win the war of asylum.

6
In Foreign Waters: Barring Escape

As the decade of the 1990s began, President George Bush proclaimed the end of the Cold War. The communist-induced refugee flows in Europe and the long-standing turmoil that had generated refugee flows in Central America seemed to be at an end. The streams of refugees from the Soviet Union and Southeast Asia who were entering the United States under the Lautenberg Amendment's softened standard of refugee eligibility were manageable. Jean-Bertrand Aristide had been democratically elected president of Haiti in December of 1990, and the Haitian exodus had ceased. But subsequent events in Haiti and Cuba soon revived the specter of floodtides of asylum seekers.

Within months of Aristide's taking office, a military junta overthrew him and once again repression, disorder, and bloodshed pervaded the country. In November of 1991, Haitians began to flee in large numbers. By the summer of 1994, as the Haitian crisis was approaching its apogee, Castro, to reduce some of the strains on his dictatorship, once again opened a Cuban harbor to mass exodus.

Washington knew that massive migrations from both Haiti and Cuba must be prevented. The elements of the established troika of interests—foreign policy, pressure groups, and costs of resettlement—that had long driven refugee and asylum policy, were in flux. The troika was no longer dominated by a foreign policy fixated on defeating communism. With no clear focus for foreign policy, the domestic demands for control and containment, stalked by a fear of floodtides, took precedence. Fear of floodtides governed policy considerations. The fear of uncontrolled migratory waves of Haitians and Cubans was reinforced by another aspect of domestic policy, the widespread and vigorous resurgence of anti-immigrant sentiment.

Pressure groups, usually in tandem with foreign policy, also were in flux. Pro-Haitian pressure groups now included the important Congressional Black Caucus, which President Clinton could not ignore; President Aristide, now in exile in Washington; and his vocal spokespersons, lawyer Ira Kurzban and former representative Michael Barnes. Human rights groups and a well-publicized hunger strike by activist Randall Robinson kept events in Haiti before the public. In contrast, the powerful Cuban American National Foundation (CANF), with its ties to the Democratic administration diminished, no longer spoke monolithically for Cuban-Americans. Newer Cuban-American groups took more flexible positions toward Castro.

The cost of refugees, which for years had been a secondary element in the troika, now assumed a greater role. While the national economy was uncertain, with growing budget deficits, the education, health, and public welfare costs of resettling mass numbers of Haitians and Cubans were perceived to be fearsome. Before the Haitian and Cuban mass escapes, Florida had estimated the costs to the state and localities for noncitizens, documented and undocumented aliens, for fiscal year 1993 at over $2.5 billion.[1] In addition to financial costs, there was the political response to be calculated. At stake were Florida's important electoral votes in the 1996 election. The public in general, and Floridians specifically, viewed immigrants and escapees as unwelcome intruders. The Clinton administration, always sensitive to public sentiment, had to factor the political response into its asylum policies.

At the core of the rearranged troika of interests was the political reality that American voters were hostile to the migrant tide. Hostility against immigrants in the 1990s reached its highest level since the heyday of nativism in the 1920s. A *Newsweek* poll in 1993 disclosed that 60 percent of Americans thought immigration bad for the country; 62 percent worried that immigrants would take jobs away from native-born workers; 59 percent believed "many " immigrants wind up on welfare; and 66 percent agreed that immigrants maintain their national identity strongly and that the United States was no longer a melting pot.[2] Some months after the *Newsweek* poll, a *New York Times/CBS News* poll revealed similar findings. When asked if immigration should be kept at its present level, increased or decreased, 61 percent preferred a decrease. One respondent was succinct: "I saw the amount of aid that went out to them [immigrants] and the way that it was abused. I feel that our economy is in a bad state and we should take care of our own."[3] A Times Mirror Center for the People and the Press survey found the American electorate to be worried about their own financial difficulties, less compassionate about the problems of the poor and minorities, and resentful toward immigrants.[4]

The time-worn restrictionist arguments, always a manifestation of economic insecurity, are again being heard. The changing economy of the 1990s has fostered anxiety about incomes and jobs. President Clinton's secretary of labor, Robert B. Reich, sees these as the concerns of "the anxious class"—"millions of Americans who no longer can count on having their jobs next year, or next month, and whose wages have stagnated or lost ground to inflation."[5] Even those who have good jobs and good salaries, when asked what the future holds for them or their children, are anxious. Their anxiety turns to anger at immigrants, refugees, and asylees.

This public angst, fed by rising taxes and a brooding national debt of trillions, has fostered a movement for federal, state, and local budgetary restraint. (At the end of 1995, federal borrowing had approached the statutory debt limit of $4.9 trillion.[6]) Restrictionists ask why citizens should subsidize health, welfare, education, and bilingual education for newcomers. Supplemental Security Income, originally intended for the native elderly poor but now supporting the parents of legal immigrants, in particular raises the hackles of restrictionists.

Allied to these economic arguments are doomsday prophesies touting the need for population limits and environmental protection and proclaiming that the United States, now a "mature" nation, has entered an era of limits. The American Immigration Control Foundation, in a small book provocatively titled *The Immigration Time Bomb,* warned that "domestic resources such as water, natural gas and timber will be rapidly depleted."[7] Donald Mann, president of Negative Population Growth, in a letter to the *New York Times* wrote:

> The debate on immigration seems to focus almost exclusively on its impact on jobs and wages. This is important, but the central issue, almost always ignored, is the degree to which immigration contributes to US population growth, and the devastating impact that growth has on our resources and environment. If left unchecked, further population growth will devastate our living standard, quality of life and environment. The driving force behind the rapid increase in our numbers is immigration, pure and simple . . . our country is already overpopulated in terms of the long-range capacity of its resources and environment.[8]

But perhaps the most pernicious arguments are those that appeal to xenophobia and racism. Xenophobes and racists, like legions of nativists before them, fear change and will not accept the fact that America's population, as a result of the Immigration Act of 1965 and of refugees, is becoming more diverse. The 1965 act, which repudiated a whites-only policy, opened immigration to people of the Eastern Hemisphere. An anticommunist foreign policy welcomed flows of escaping Nicaraguans, Cubans, and Southeast Asians. Today's newcomers are primarily people of color. Census projections foretell that by 2040 about 40 percent of the population will consist of people of color: immigrant and native-born Latinos, Asians, and blacks.

The leading anti-immigration group today is the Federation for American Immigration Reform (FAIR), the intellectual descendent of the frankly named Immigration Restriction League. FAIR runs newspaper ads head-lined "End of the Migration Era—Time for a Moratorium," which ask a series of leading questions:

- Why do we need immigration?
- Do we need more people? Are we underpopulated?
- Is there an acute labor shortage in the US?
- Are the water tables in Florida, California and Texas flooded?
- Is there an excess of prime farmland in America?
- Is there too much wildlife in our national parks?
- Is there an overabundance of beach front property to be developed?
- Do we need immigration to improve public education?
- Do we need immigration to reduce crime in America?
- Do we need immigration to improve medical care?
- Are there too many acres of wetland in need of paving?
- Are we too homogeneous to be a legitimate nation?
- Does our national security depend, in any way, on significant immigration?

FAIR answers each of these questions with a no, and then argues: "If we don't need immigration, why have it? The answer may seem to be per-ceived tradition and habit. . . . FAIR thinks the nation could use a morato-rium or time-out on immigration for a while." The ad has a dual motive: While FAIR appears to be arguing that immigrants will increase population pressures on resources and services, it also is implanting the suggestion that immigrants will degrade education, increase crime, and, most insidiously, divide the country.

The general population does not discriminate among categories of newcom-ers. Michael S. Teitelbaum and Myron Weiner have correctly observed that "all the available evidence suggests that public concern stimulated by illegal immigration has extended to legal immigration numbers, and that refugees and asylees are considered to be in the same category as legal and illegal im-migrants."[9] FAIR and the American public are calling for restriction of im-migration and refugee numbers, and elected officials are responding.

In the summer of 1995, the federal advisory Commission on Immigration Reform, headed by the late Barbara Jordan of Texas, proposed the most significant changes in immigration law in more than four decades. The commission recommended reducing legal immigration by one-third and changing the immigration preference given to close relatives of citizens (brothers, sisters, and adult children). The Jordan Commission also recom-mended reducing the number of refugees admitted, to 50,000 a year. This was a significant drop in numbers—more than 100,000 people had come in annually since 1990—at a time when the world's refugee population had reached unprecedented heights. The commission also stated, in a preliminary report to Congress, that "a credible immigration policy requires the ability to respond effectively and humanely to immigration emergencies."[10] The Haitians and Cubans had presented an "immigration emergency"; whether the United States responded "effectively and humanely" is open to debate.

Eight years earlier, in February of 1986, the United States had eased out of Haiti its dictator Jean-Claude Duvalier, flying him and his entourage into exile on a US Air Force military transport. The Duvaliers, father and son, had presided over a dominion of corruption, repression, killings, and terror. Income and wealth were vested in a tiny minority (0.8 percent of the population possessed 44.8 percent of the wealth),[11] and the political system protected and maintained their privilege.

The Duvaliers were gone, but their legacy of terror and privation remained. The Haitian people suffered under three different military dictatorships, a short-lived civilian puppet regime, and an unstable and weak provisional government. The provisional government, however, sought and received extensive international monitoring and assistance from the United Nations and the Organization of American States to ensure Haiti's first free and fair elections. On December 16, 1990, elections were held for president, and over 67 percent of the vote was given to Father Jean-Bertrand Aristide, a popular and populist Roman Catholic priest who had survived two assassination attempts by Duvalierist thugs. But Duvalierism was not yet dead.[12]

Before Aristide assumed the presidency, a former tontons macoutes chief attempted to overthrow the government. The coup failed, largely because the army was swayed by a massive popular protest and the warnings of foreign embassies not to back the Duvalierists.[13] On February 7, 1991, Aristide became Haiti's first leader to be popularly elected in this century. He soon attempted structural reform. He tried to reshape the army, retiring generals and transferring officers notorious for human rights abuses to obscure posts. Colonel Raoul Cedras, who had headed the election security committee, was promoted and named interim commander-in-chief. Aristide also abolished the section chiefs who had, through violence and extortion, turned rural Haiti into a collection of personal fiefdoms. Aristide attempted to improve the prisons, to document past human rights abuses, to separate the police force from the army, and to reform the corrupt and inept bureaucracy.[14] But his attempts at reform were short lived. Within the year he had been deposed by a coup. Amy Wilentz, an astute observer of Haiti, has succinctly summarized the situation:

Aristide's program of moderate but adamant social reform has earned him the undying hatred of Haiti's economic elite, a clique that despises democracy and that historically has manipulated the army. This coup is the military expression of the elite's ardent refusal to share economic and political power with the Haitian people.[15]

With Aristide forced out of the country, repression returned. During Aristide's short tenure, the number of Haitians seeking refuge in the United States had dropped dramatically; there were months in which the Coast Guard did not encounter a single Haitian boat.[16] But with the promise of Aristide dashed, Haitians again took to their boats. Within six months after the coup, the US Coast Guard had intercepted more than 38,000 Haitians. In the three years following Aristide's ouster, some 68,500 Haitians fled in small boats; another 30,000 found refuge, sometimes a harsh refuge, in the Dominican Republic; more than 300,000 Haitians were displaced within their own country.[17]

The Bush administration responded to the new exodus with its old policy: interdiction, cursory asylum hearings on board Coast Guard vessels with inadequately trained asylum officers, and repatriation. Haitian advocates sued, asserting that the government asylum screenings were unfair. The number of fleeing Haitians climbed. As shipboard screening became impractical, the government began transferring interdicted Haitians to Guantanamo Naval Base. From Guantanamo, those found not eligible to apply for asylum in the United States were returned, most of them involuntarily, to Haiti.

When they reached Port-au-Prince, the returned Haitians, adults and children, were fingerprinted, questioned, and photographed by uniformed Haitians. US officials turned over to the military junta the ships' manifests with the name, age, and hometown of each returnee. Sadako Ogata, the United Nations High Commissioner for Refugees, was openly critical of the procedure:

Continuing reports of serious human rights abuses and violence by security forces since the overthrow of the democratically elected government of Haiti are cause for great concern. For this reason, UNHCR fears that those being returned may, in fact, be exposed to danger upon their return.[18]

Despite the danger of repatriation, thousands of Haitians jammed into small, unseaworthy boats seeking a reprieve from their persecution and misery. The already impoverished life of the great mass of Haitians was worsening. The Bush administration, in an attempt to oust the junta that had deposed Aristide, had persuaded the Organization of American States to impose a hemispheric embargo against Haiti. It was thought that if most of the country's exports and imports were cut off, the military and the wealthy businessmen who supported them would be forced to accept a brokered compromise, permitting Aristide to return. But the military and the elite feared Aristide more than they feared the sanctions.

The embargo failed. European countries ignored it; other countries by-passed it. The administration was unwilling to enforce the embargo with a naval blockade, nor would it cut the transportation links that permitted wealthy Haitians to fly to Miami and other consumer paradises and return with suitcases loaded with embargoed goods. A National Council of Churches of Christ delegation to Haiti reported: "It is clear that the embargo is having little practical effect except to aggravate the situation of Haiti's poor majority. The main impact of the embargo has been to double prices. We observed plentiful supplies of gas, well-stocked supermarkets, ships in the port and docks crowded with containers."[19] The working poor and the peasants suffered most. It was calculated that more than 40,000 people who assembled goods for re-export lost their jobs.[20] At least 150,000 people were estimated to be out of work.[21]

Walter Fauntroy, the District of Columbia congressman who was for many years chairman of the congressional task force on Haiti, described the effects of the embargo on the peasants:

> The peasants who used to make a few dollars selling mangoes, peppers, cocoa or vegetables to US exporters are now forced to sell for a quarter of the old price to the Dominicans, who then sell to the US exporters. The oil embargo has limited electrical power and shut down the rural irrigation facil-ities. I've had reports that even the mango trees are being cut down and used for charcoal for cooking. The only industry on the island now is drug trans-shipment and boat-building.
>
> We're not punishing the military; we're punishing the peasants—forcing them to flee and then sending them right back to starve.[22]

Under pressure from American businesses that were losing money, some months after the embargo began the Bush administration permitted Ameri-can corporations to resume operations. This change in policy heartened the military dictatorship and its supporters, but it did not discourage the exodus. Washington was concerned that rescuing Haitians from their flimsy boats only encouraged departures.

The Guantanamo Naval Base, by the end of May 1992, was at capacity and its water, electrical, and sewage systems overburdened. Nearly 12,500 refugees were living in tents, some for more than six months. The INS had tripled its staff of asylum officers to more than one hundred. These officers, part of the newly trained asylum corps, were prescreening refugees, sending on to the States those who seemed to have a credible basis for making an asylum claim. To the dismay of the State Department, which continued to insist that the departing Haitians were leaving for economic and not for political reasons, by the end of May 1992, about 10,300 of some 36,600 interdicted Haitians screened at Guantanamo had been sent on to the United States to pursue their asylum claims.[23]

Suddenly shifting its policy, the administration ordered the Coast Guard to stop interdicting boats and pick up only vessels judged to be in imminent danger of sinking. The embargo was being felt not by the ruling elite but by the masses of poor Haitians; the junta remained entrenched while the boat people fled. Officials from the State Department, the Immigration and Naturalization Service, and the Pentagon met at the White House to consider new policy options.[24] Politics tinged the discussions: The presidential elections were only six months away, and southern Florida must not be overwhelmed by Haitian boat people. On Memorial Day weekend, from his vacation home in Kennebunkport, Maine, President Bush issued an executive order.

The Kennebunkport Order ended *all* asylum screenings. Every Haitian interdicted at sea would be forcibly returned, without even an interview, to Haiti. President Bush insisted that the draconian policy was "necessary to save the lives of the Haitians."[25] Campaigning in Georgia, he was asked if his new policy seemed "to stand counter to what America has stood for over the last couple of hundred years." The president responded: "Yes, the Statue of Liberty still stands, and we still open our arms under our law to people that are politically oppressed. I will not, because I've sworn to uphold the Constitution, open the doors to economic refugees all over the world. We can't do that." Barbara Crossette, reporting for the *New York Times,* noted that the crowd applauded.[26]

Others thought differently. Governor Bill Clinton of Arkansas, soon to be the Democratic presidential nominee, declared that he was "appalled by the decision of the Bush Administration to pick up fleeing Haitians on the high seas and forcibly return them to Haiti before considering their claim to political asylum." He went on to say:

> It was bad enough when there were failures to offer them due process in making such a claim. Now they are offered no process at all before being returned.
> This policy must not stand. It is a blow to the principle of first asylum and to America's moral authority in defending the rights of refugees around the world. This most recent policy shift is another sad example of the Administration's callous response to a terrible human tragedy. . . .
> If I were president, I would—in the absence of clear and compelling evidence that they weren't political refugees—give them temporary asylum here until we restored the elected government of Haiti.[27]

Arthur Helton, then the director of the refugee project of the Lawyers

Committee for Human Rights, called Bush's order a "gross violation of international law."[28] John G. Healey, executive director of Amnesty International USA, expressed the views of human rights groups, international lawyers, and Haitian advocates when he said:

> The United States Government is now acting as gate keeper for the repressive forces in Haiti.
> In much the same way as the Berlin Wall prevented Germans from leaving East Berlin, our government is effectively building a Caribbean Curtain to keep Haitians in Haiti and out of the United States.
> Telling the Coast Guard to return Haitian refugees to Haiti is like telling fire fighters to escort people back to a burning building.[29]

Refugee advocates compared the policy to the ill-fated voyage of the *St. Louis* and vowed to challenge it in Congress and the courts. Congressional critics deplored the policy but could not muster the votes to change it. Some opponents of the policy pointed out that the Bush administration had objected when Britain returned Vietnamese boat people arriving in Hong Kong. UN officials said that the policy violated international agreements and warned that there would be dire consequences if other countries followed the example of the United States.[30]

When Clinton took office, Haitians at all levels expected that he would initiate a change of policy. The night Clinton was elected, Haitians in the slums of Port-au Prince rejoiced and danced in the streets. A few Haitians managed to elude the Coast Guard patrols that ringed the island; shortly after the election, customs agents discovered sixty-two Haitian stowaways aboard a rickety freighter on the Miami River. *The Economist* reported that "eighteen refugees, most of them women, were in a compartment 13 feet long and three feet high filled with fumes from the engine room."[31] The stowaways were anticipating a more generous welcome than had been proffered by the Bush administration. Yet the vast majority of Haitians, even had the door been open, could not have paid for the trip. As the repression in Haiti worsened, boat owners raised their fares, up to $700; Haitians earned on the average $100 a year.

The stowaways were not the only ones who had anticipated a change in policy. A Church World Service newsletter observed, "As a candidate, and as president-elect, Clinton has made clear that he intends to change United States policy toward Haitian refugees when he becomes president." Church World Service and sixteen other national labor, religious, and human rights organizations wrote to Clinton's transition team, suggesting a new policy of expanded in-country refugee processing, an end to automatic repatriation, the opening of a safe haven in the Caribbean, temporary protected status for

Haitians in the United States, and a settlement of legal challenges to Bush's Kennebunkport Order.[32]

Other organizations too believed that Clinton's election signaled a change. The Carnegie Endowment for International Peace held a roundtable on Haitian Migration Policy. The invitation was signed by Doris M. Meissner, who would become Clinton's commissioner of the Immigration and Naturalization Service, and indicated that among the participants would be someone from the presidential transition team, the director of the State Department's Bureau of Refugee Programs, and others involved in formulating immigration and refugee policy.

The discussion draft suggested a number of principles to guide US policy. It recognized that the Haitian migration could not be categorized simply but comprised "convention refugees, people seeking safety from violence, and those searching for a better life." It urged international action, rather than unilateral action by the United States. The draft recommended that the root causes of the migration from Haiti be addressed, restoring democracy in Haiti and improving conditions there. The embargo, it argued, was "simply hurting the poor and profiting the elites." It recommended that the embargo be either lifted or strengthened, so that "it bites those whose acquiescence is required for a political solution." Within Haiti, the draft suggested a stronger presence of human rights monitors from the OAS, "particularly in the countryside where section chiefs are responsible for the majority of abuses."

In two other areas, the document made important proposals. First, it enjoined that:

> The principle of non-refoulement must be observed. Though the Supreme Court may rule that the 1951 Refugee Convention does not apply on the high seas, the US should behave according to the spirit of refugee doctrine. This is particularly important today. Many countries will be guided by the standards the US sets in response to changing international conditions that create emergency migrations.

That principle could best be preserved by having the UN High Commissioner for Refugees establish safe havens within the region. Once these were in place the Kennebunkport Order should be revoked. Finally, the document recommended that Haitians who had been admitted to the United States from Guantanamo within the previous year should be given temporary protected status.[33]

Sadako Ogata, the UN High Commissioner for Refugees, and Grover Joseph Rees III, general counsel of the Immigration and Naturalization Service, also presented the Clinton transition team with proposals for dealing with the Haitian exodus. The UNHCR drafted a proposal for countries throughout the Western Hemisphere to grant temporary asylum to Haitian boat people. Rees proposed "refugee processing at a protected enclave either in Haiti or in some third country" or, alternatively, holding asylum hearings on board ship or at Guantanamo.[34]

Whatever policy options lay before the transition team were shadowed by fears of a mass exodus from Haiti. In the weeks before Clinton's inauguration, there were widespread media reports of massive boat building on Haiti's shores. Bush administration officials estimated (wrongly, it turned out) that 200,000 to 500,000 Haitians would attempt to leave the island.[35] (FAIR repeatedly ran radio spots in Florida and Georgia warning of a massive and inevitable influx of Haitians.) Believing that the United States faced a mass migration from Haiti, a crisis of both foreign and domestic policy, Clinton jettisoned his campaign promises. Before his inauguration, Clinton made a radio address to the Haitian people in which he warned: "Those who do leave Haiti directly by boat will be stopped and directly returned by the United States Coast Guard."[36] The *New York Times* editorialized that Clinton's "official explanation for reversing himself is to avoid the humanitarian catastrophe of capsized boats and overcrowded camps. . . . But Mr. Clinton's real worry appears to be political fallout in Florida in reaction to a flood of poor black Haitian refugees."[37]

The returned boat people, with their right to request asylum denied, were given only one way to escape to the United States: They could apply for refugee status through the in-country processing (ICP) program within Haiti. In-country processing programs had been used in Vietnam, Cuba, and the former Soviet Union.

In-country processing was inadequate at best. The number of Haitians admitted for refugee resettlement by the United States—54 in fiscal year 1992; 1,307 in fiscal year 1993—was inordinately low for a country with an abysmal and continuing disregard for human rights. An American Immigration Lawyers Association investigation concluded, "Repression in Haiti is rampant and . . . it is of a uniquely political nature."[38] A church group stated, "The vast majority of Haitians continue to live in a climate of fear and insecurity. Extrajudicial executions, arbitrary detention, torture, threats and intimidation are routine."[39] Many observers were critical. One careful study, *No Port in a Storm: The Misguided Use of In-Country Refugee Processing in Haiti,* documented significant shortcomings in the program.[40] Haitians who applied placed themselves at risk and received no protection. The risks worsened with the long period of waiting for a decision. Moreover, the only way for a Haitian to apply was through a written questionnaire, but the great majority of Haitians were illiterate. Finally, the decisions reached seemed unfair and inconsistent.

In an attempt to reduce the overall numbers, the standards for in-country processing were revised, but only to make them more stringent. Only senior and mid-level government officials under Aristide, associates of Aristide, and high-level professionals, such as journalists—in essence, only the prominent or the visible—could appear for an interview. As Haiti rapidly deteriorated into a state of chaos, at the end of July 1994, commercial flights from Haiti were halted. More than one thousand Haitians who had been accepted for resettlement in the United States were left stranded inside the country.[41]

In the long term, Clinton wanted "the reinstatement of the legitimate and democratically elected government of President Aristide." He hoped to achieve this by continuing the diplomatic efforts begun by the Bush administration together with the UN and the Organization of American States to bring about a negotiated political settlement.[42] To prevent the immediate crisis of a potential mass exodus from Haiti, he set up Operation Able Manner, surrounding Haiti with twenty-two ships and deploying planes and helicopters for surveillance. Clinton was now enforcing the Kennebunkport Order, the order that he had previously denounced as "illegal and immoral." Clinton's repatriation policy evoked the same responses as when it had been initiated by Bush. Refugee advocates and human rights organizations deplored it as a violation of human rights and international law. Others viewed it as an appropriate response to deter economic migrants.

The United States was now in a diplomatically anomalous position, working with the UN to restore democratic government to Haiti while enforcing a policy of refoulement to which the UN was adamantly opposed. Clinton was forced to defend that decision in the courts. The case, ultimately designated as *Sale v. Haitian Centers Council,* was argued before the Supreme Court by Professor Harold Hongju Koh of the Yale University Law School.

Koh believed the Kennebunkport Order "constituted a textbook case of refoulement, for it effectively erected a 'floating Berlin Wall' around Haiti that prevented Haitians from fleeing anywhere, not just to the United States."[43] Koh's main brief was supported by an affidavit of Columbia University Professor Louis Henkin, who, as a State Department representative, had helped draft the Refugee Convention. Henkin concluded his affidavit with a clear understanding of what the drafters of the convention had meant: "A state could not seize a refugee in its territory and hand him over to his oppressors. It may not—indeed, *a fortiori*—reach out beyond its borders, pick up a refugee off the high seas and forcibly return him into the hands of his oppressors."[44] Amicus briefs were filed for such organizations as Americas Watch, Amnesty International, the NAACP, the Association of the Bar of the City of New York, the Lawyers' Committee for Human Rights, and the UNHCR. Professor Deborah Anker of the Harvard Immigration Clinic submitted a brief on behalf of members of Congress that analyzed the legislative history of the Refugee Act. Professor David Martin of the University of Virginia School of Law submitted a "Brandeis brief" recounting how the United States had responded more generously to other refugees.[45]

Notwithstanding these arguments, the Supreme Court held the Kennebunkport Order to be legal. Writing for the eight-to-one majority, Associate Justice John Paul Stevens found that the protections against forced repatriation of refugees apply "only to aliens who reside or have arrived at the border of the United States." The lone dissenter, Associate Justice Harry Blackmun, took sharp issue with his brethren. He wrote:

> Today's majority . . . decides that the forced repatriation of the Haitian refugees is perfectly legal because the word "return" does not mean return, because the opposite of "within the United States" is not outside the United States, and because the official charged with controlling immigration has no role in enforcing an order to control immigration. . . .
> What is extraordinary in this case is that the Executive, in disregard of the law, would take to the seas to intercept fleeing refugees and force them back to their persecutors—and that the Court would strain to sanction that conduct.[46]

Koh observed, "In the end, Haitian Centers Council will be remembered as a narrow, apologetic opinion that validated a uniquely discriminatory interdiction program."[47] The UN High Commissioner for Refugees was far more critical, stating that the decision was "a setback to modern international refugee law which has been developing for more than forty years, since the end of World War II. It renders the work of the Office of the High Commissioner in its global refugee protection role more difficult and sets a very unfortunate example."[48]

Within two weeks of the Supreme Court's decision, the Clinton administration began to move toward a political settlement and, after protracted and intense negotiations, succeeded in brokering an accord between President Aristide and General Cedras. Under the Governors Island Accord, Aristide would appoint a prime minister; trade sanctions would be lifted after the prime minister's appointment but before Aristide returned to Haiti. In addition, multinational forces would train the Haitian army and create a new police force; coup leaders would retire from the government, and the military junta would be granted amnesty for crimes committed while in office. The accord never came to fruition.

The military regime, in an attempt to eliminate support for Aristide, redoubled its efforts to terrorize: Human rights violations soared; Aristide's supporters and cabinet ministers were murdered. Shortly before Aristide was scheduled to return to Haiti, in October 1993, the USS *Harlan County* attempted to dock at Port-au-Prince. The ship, carrying a contingent of United States and Canadian personnel, the vanguard of a UN mission to oversee the restoration of Aristide, was met at the dock by demonstrators waving machetes and yelling: "We are going to make this another Somalia!"[49] The ship was ordered to retreat. The Governors Island Accord had collapsed, leaving the junta in power.

The United States had been defied and humiliated by Haiti's generals, yet the Clinton administration continued to direct that Aristide share power with the junta. During the first months of 1994, the administration asked that Aristide make concessions to the coup leaders; but the administration discounted the reign of terror conducted by the army-backed paramilitary group, the Front for the Advancement and Progress of Haiti (FRAPH). FRAPH's leader, Emmanuel Constant, it was later revealed, was on the payroll of the CIA. A *New York Times* editorial noted: "Government officials confirm he was paid by the agency and kept in close touch with it at a time when he was doing his best to prevent the return to Haiti of its ousted President, Jean-Bertrand Aristide." The editorial continued: "It is abundantly clear that the CIA did not play a constructive role in Haiti policy."[50]

The administration's Haiti policy was stalemated. Domestic pressures demanded that the policy be changed. In March 1994, the Congressional Black Caucus, with the support of liberals, introduced a bill in the House of Representatives to tighten the economic embargo against Haiti, terminate commercial flights to and from the United States, block Haitian financial assets held in the United States, and stop the summary return of Haitian asylum seekers interdicted at sea. A similar bill was introduced in the Senate. Although the bills were never put to a vote, together they had more than seventy-five sponsors, pressure Clinton found hard to ignore. In April, President Aristide announced that the interdiction agreement would terminate in six months. When Randall Robinson, the executive director of the lobbying group TransAfrica Forum, went on a well-publicized hunger strike to protest the treatment of the Haitians, the administration buckled. During the spring and summer, it began to shape a new policy. Ultimately, all of the measures advocated by the Black Caucus would be carried out.

Pressure was increased on the military regime. The United States secured a UN resolution to widen the embargo and enforce it with stiffer sanctions. (The only exceptions were to be food, medicine, and propane cooking gas.) And Clinton even hinted that he might use force to eject the junta and restore Aristide. Haitians interdicted at sea would not be forcibly repatriated but would have their claims for refugee status adjudicated. Haitians picked up at sea were sent for processing to a US hospital ship anchored off the coast of Jamaica. In the first few weeks, nearly a third of those who applied received refugee status, an approval level equal to that from 1991–92. By the end of June, more than 10,000 boat people had been picked up, the highest level in two years. Confronted by the sheer numbers of this new exodus, in early July the Clinton administration once again shifted course.

The again revised policy decreed that refugees intercepted at sea would no longer be resettled in the United States but would be sent to safe havens in the Caribbean.[51] But negotiations with countries in the region to provide these havens failed, and Haitians were sent instead to Guantanamo; they were not, however, to be processed on Guantanamo for refugee status. Haitians could seek refuge in the United States only through the flawed in-country processing procedure.

There seemed but one way out of the Haitian crisis—to remove Cedras and company. At the end of July, the United States obtained a UN resolution permitting it, together with a multinational force, "to use all necessary means to facilitate the departure from Haiti of the military leadership."[52] But Cedras would not negotiate meaningfully.

In response to Cedras's recalcitrance, the Department of State issued, on September 13, a third interim report on "Human Rights in Haiti." In a presage of a major policy change and a marked departure from past country reports, the new report gave credence to what independent human rights observers had maintained for years. The report concluded:

> The human rights situation in Haiti under the illegal Cedras regime is comparable to the notorious regime of François "Papa Doc" Duvalier. The military and the de facto government promote repression and terror, sanctioning widespread assassination, killing, torture, beating, mutilation and rape. The regime's actions openly defy the international community, which has repeatedly condemned these gross human rights violations.[53]

Two days after the State Department released its report, President Clinton addressed the nation to explain why military intervention was needed:

> Thousands of Haitians have already fled toward the United States risking their lives to escape the reign of terror. As long as Cedras rules, Haitians will continue to seek sanctuary in our nation. This year, in less than two months, more than 21,000 Haitians were rescued at sea by our Coast Guard and Navy. Today, more than 14,000 refugees are living at our naval base in Guantanamo. The American people have already expended almost $200 million to support them, to maintain the economic embargo, and the prospect of

millions more being spent every month for an indefinite period of time looms ahead unless we act. Three hundred thousand more Haitians, 5 percent of their entire population, are hiding in their own country. If we don't act, they could be the next wave of refugees at our door. We will continue to face the threat of a mass exodus of refugees and its constant threat to stability in our region, and control of our borders.[54]

Military intervention, the most extreme weapon in the arsenal of foreign policy, was to be invoked. Domestic pressures—the fear of a continuing exodus, the need to assert control of our borders, lobbying on behalf of Aristide—and the threat of enormous costs had together taken control of the refugee admissions troika.

In a last desperate move to avoid an unpopular invasion, Clinton authorized former president Jimmy Carter, Senator Sam Nunn, and retired general Colin Powell to negotiate with the junta. On September 18, as planes were already en route to Haiti, the Carter delegation contrived an accord. Under the agreement, the three top coup leaders would step down, after which the Haitian Parliament would pass a general amnesty, and international sanctions would be lifted. Despite the "gross human rights violations" committed by the despots, they were to receive lavish compensation for their departure. "Hours after forcing Haiti's military leaders into exile," the *New York Times* reported, "the White House announced a series of rewards today for them and their associates. The rewards included safe passage for family members to the United States, an agreement to rent three houses in Haiti from them, and access to at least $79 million in frozen bank accounts."[55]

The day after the agreement, American military personnel, without a shot having been fired, occupied Haiti, the advance guard of a UN force. On October 15, jubilant crowds welcomed Aristide back to Haiti. In the United States, the National Coalition for Haitian Refugees, the leading Haitian advocacy group in the United States, changed its name to the National Coalition for Haitian Rights.[56] In Haiti, civil society reemerged. Order was guaranteed first by a US-led multinational force and then by the presence of over six thousand United Nations Mission in Haiti (UNMIH) peacekeepers and over eight hundred UN Civilian Police monitors.[57] Under the protective aegis of the UN and the OAS, Aristide was able to complete the remainder of his term, and a year after the invasion free elections were held. In April 1996, the last American troops with the United Nations peacekeeping mission departed Haiti. Only a humanitarian mission of 250 American troops remained behind to help build schools, hospitals, and roads.[58] The Clinton administration could proclaim its Haiti policy a resounding success: The mass escape of Haitians had been stanched, the repressive regime had been ousted, and Aristide's successor had been chosen in a free democratic election.

Aristide's successor, René Préval, has the daunting task of social, economic, and political reconstruction. Given its long history of despotic governments and its inexperience in democratic rule, Haiti will require significant and continuing international protection and aid. Without them, another mass exodus is virtually certain.

Haiti's neighbor, Cuba, also could create a mass exodus crisis. It has already done so several times: first in the early 1960s, after Castro's takeover; then in 1965, with the opening of the port of Camarioca; in 1980, with the Mariel boatlift; and amid the Haitian crisis in the summer of 1994.

Through the earlier crises, the United States welcomed all Cubans. Until the summer of 1994. Until then, policy had followed the seemingly immutable troika of interests. American foreign policy was steadfastly anticommunist, and Castro personified the threat of communism. Cuba, the State Department repeatedly warned, was "the key Soviet proxy."[59] *The Soviet-Cuban Connection in Central America and the Caribbean,* a State Department/Defense Department booklet replete with maps, graphs, and photos, documented the menace. If the CIA could not rid the hemisphere of Castro by assassination, or invasion, we could strangle his island's economy with an embargo. We could also embarrass him by encouraging and welcoming defectors.

Anticommunist foreign policy was encouraged by support from Cuban-Americans. Politically and economically powerful in Florida and metropolitan New York–New Jersey, the Cuban-Americans spoke with one anti-Castro voice. To offend them was to risk great political cost. But the Mariel crisis wreaked political and economic havoc: the inundations had been disorderly, resettlement chaotic, costs high; blacks and anglos resented the newly arrived Cubans; criminals had remained in prison for years; receiving communities resented shouldering burdens they felt belonged to the federal government; blacks and refugee advocates resented the blatant disparity of treatment of Haitians and Cubans; there had been a strong anti-immigrant reaction. Politicians rapidly learned the lesson of Mariel: Mass escapes must not be permitted. But Castro too had learned the lesson of Mariel.

In the summer of 1994, while the United States worked to remove Cedras and company from Haiti, Castro once again flung open his doors, condoning another mass escape. Washington would not repeat the earlier policy responses of Mariel. Nonetheless, its responses in 1994, as in Mariel, were characterized by indecision, sudden shifts in policy, the ultimate admission of large numbers of Cubans, and an ad hoc resolution of the crisis that allowed Castro to attain his goals.

As in the Mariel exodus, the new exodus was precipitated by long-term conditions. Daily life under Castro had become ever more burdensome.

There was neither free speech nor a free press. Laws banned "enemy propaganda" and clandestine printing. The state owned the media. Dissidents, critics, and opponents of the government were imprisoned. For the crime of offending the president, a Cuban could be jailed for three years. Nor was there free political expression. No civic or political groups independent of the government or the Communist party were legally recognized. Courts were not independent. State security police monitored daily life. Ubiquitous Committees for the Defense of the Revolution operated in workplaces and neighborhoods throughout the island, enforcing conformity and "socialist morality." To political repression was added economic hardship.[60]

Cuba was in an economic slide. With the demise of the Union of Soviet Socialist Republics and the Soviet bloc, the favorable trade arrangements and subsidies bestowed on Cuba had disappeared. The managed economy was mismanaged. And the long-term US blockade added to the country's distress. Cuba was suffering its most severe economic crisis since Castro came to power. Tightened food rationing led to scarcity of basic foodstuffs; soap, rum, and cooking oil became rare luxuries. Normal life was hampered by fuel shortages and electric blackouts.[61]

Before the full force of economic hardship hit, Cuban arrivals to Florida had been manageable—391 in 1989 and 467 in 1990. But as the standard of living declined, the number of Cubans risking their lives and the penalties for "illegal departure" climbed rapidly. For the next four years, the numbers tell the story: 2,203 in 1991; 2,608 in 1992; 3,881 in 1993; and 5,779 from the beginning of 1994 until a few days before Castro sanctioned the opening of the floodgates in mid-August.[62]

US policy makers, bound by a foreign policy of anti-Castro communism and supported in their myopia by Cuban-American pressure groups, were heedless of the portent of rising numbers of *balseros,* escapees on makeshift boats and rafts. For the State Department, the Cold War might be over in Europe, but at our doorstep, Cuba remained a mocking nemesis. To the Cuban American National Foundation, the powerful Cuban-American lobby, a policy of economic strangulation of Cuba would hasten Castro's downfall.

CANF was founded in 1980 by Jorge Mas Canosa, who had arrived in Miami as a penniless refugee and become a multimillionaire. The foundation has donated more than one million dollars to congressional and presidential candidates,[63] and its directors, individually, have contributed enormous sums to politicians. CANF has been described as "a millionaires' club of right-wing exiles with a hefty war chest."[64] Its first success was the establishment of Radio Martí during the Reagan administration. CANF's political muscle is so strong that one Bush administration official was quoted as saying: "The foundation has a chilling effect on the debate. Anytime anyone starts to think creatively about Cuba we're told: What do you want to do, lose South Florida for us?"[65]

The fear of losing South Florida permeated both the Bush and the Clinton campaigns in 1992. A year earlier, Robert Torricelli, a Democratic congressman from a New Jersey district with a large Cuban constituency, introduced the Cuban Democracy Act (CDA) to expand the embargo that had been imposed in 1963 at the height of the Cold War.

The Bush administration had initially opposed the CDA because it barred foreign subsidiaries operating in the United States from trading with Cuba. (This was of dubious international legality and damaging to relations with American allies.) Bill Clinton's advisers on Latin America also counseled opposing the bill. But Clinton, needing campaign funds, and the blessing of Mas Canosa, endorsed the CDA, saying, "I think [the Bush] administration has missed a big opportunity to put the hammer down on Fidel Castro and Cuba." Shortly thereafter, the Clinton campaign raised $275,000 in South Florida. A Clinton campaign official observed that "good politics makes bad policy." President Bush too had to endorse the CDA. The bill was signed into law two weeks before the elections. Three weeks after Clinton won the presidency, the United Nations General Assembly voted to support a nonbinding Cuban resolution condemning the embargo.[66]

Clinton won the presidency, but he lost Florida. CANF's funding helped the campaign, but the Cuban vote could not deliver the state. Clinton's initial Cuban policy was, according to Cuba expert Gillian Gunn, "a contradictory, ambivalent course, displaying hard-line tendencies and sensitivity to conservative Cuban-American concerns interspersed with evidence of 'new thinking.'"[67] In a 1993 Twentieth Century Fund Paper, *Cuba in Transition: Options for US Policy,* Ms. Gunn prophetically wrote: "It is plausible that Cuba policy will continue to drift until some crisis occurs on the island, finally forcing Washington to make decisions. By then, having neglected long-term planning and policy reappraisal in the interest of short-term political expediency, Washington may only be able to choose from among the least of several evils."[68] When, in August of 1994, Castro presented the Clinton administration with another crisis of mass escape, the options available to policy makers in Washington were limited.

Clinton administration policy makers, although preoccupied with resolving the Haitian crisis, nonetheless had known long before the summer of 1994 that discontent was rising in Cuba. The numbers of balseros rose each month: in January, 266; February, 410; March, 532; April, 768; May, 783; June, 1,176; July, 1,312. Moreover, in the spring of 1994, the events that had presaged the Mariel exodus were being uncannily replayed. In May and

June, some 150 Cubans sought asylum on the grounds of foreign missions. Then, in July and August, events took a dramatic turn.

On July 13, seventy-two Cubans hijacked a state-owned tugboat and headed it out of the Havana harbor into the open sea. Government boats intercepted the tug, sprayed it with high-pressure water cannons, then rammed it. The tug sank, and thirty-seven people, some of them children, died.[69] A hijacking of a ferry on July 26 was more successful. Half of the thirty people on board were taken by the Coast Guard to the United States; the others chose to return to Cuba.[70] On August 3, eighty Cubans hijacked a Havana ferry with nearly two hundred passengers on board. Cuban patrol boats pursued the ferry and captured it when it ran out of fuel. With the earlier tugboat tragedy still fresh, Cuban authorities notified the US Coast Guard of the ferry's location and permitted those who wished to leave for the United States to do so. The eighty who planned the escape were joined by thirty-seven ferry passengers.

Up to that point, the hijackings had been nonviolent. But on August 4, when a group tried to hijack a ferry, a Cuban policeman was killed. On August 5, police tried to prevent a group of Cubans from launching a raft; crowds turned on the police, seized their weapons, killed two policemen and injured another. In downtown Havana, thousands of people spontaneously rioted and chanted antigovernment slogans in "the largest expression of antigovernment sentiment since the 1959 revolution brought Castro to power."[71] After the riot, Castro cracked down on dissidents, and hundreds of people were arrested.

On August 6, at a news conference, Castro spoke about the United States' "ploy of preventing legal immigration and encouraging illegal emigration." He warned that "if the United States fails to adopt immediate and efficient measures to stop the encouragement of illegal departures from our country, we will be dutybound to instruct our coast guards [sic] not to intercept any boat leaving Cuba."[72] The State Department responded with hubris: "The United States has stated repeatedly that we will not permit Fidel Castro to dictate our immigration policy or to create a replay of the Mariel boat lift, a cynical move on the part of Castro. . . . We urge the Cuban Government to carefully consider all the implications of such incitement. We urge the citizens of Cuba and their relatives in the United States to remain calm and not to participate in this ploy of the Cuban Government."[73] On August 8, twenty-one Cubans commandeered a boat to the United States and killed a Cuban naval officer.

On August 11, the *New York Times,* in an editorial evocatively titled "Cubans, and Cuba Policy, Lost at Sea," suggested a change in American policy that might have averted the mass exodus crisis:

> The US is trapped in a self-made dilemma. . . .
> American's Cuban policy has been frozen in the past, kept there by Presidents pandering to the most fanatical faction of the exile community in Florida. The humane and sensible way for the US to avert a new Mariel is to ease sanctions, lift un-American curbs on travel to Cuba and permit more Cubans to immigrate legally, in return for a measure of political liberalization for the islanders. If a deal along these lines were offered to Fidel Castro, he would run the risk of opposition more serious than sporadic riots.[74]

On August 12, the Cuban Coast Guard was formally ordered not to apprehend Cubans leaving the country unless they attempted to do so in a stolen boat. On August 13, Castro publicly blamed the United States for the rioting and hijackings. He threatened that, if the United States did not take steps to deter boat departures and return hijackers who committed violent acts, he would open his doors. For Castro, flinging open the doors of exit was a well-tried safety measure to reduce discontent and prevent the growth of opposition movements. Camarioca and Mariel had worked to his advantage. Now Castro would permit the most disaffected to depart; his agents would force out others.[75]

Washington ignored the warnings, and Havana opened the floodgates. Cubans flocked to the beaches, and in makeshift rafts, inner tubes, and small boats set out to sea. The US Navy and Coast Guard, which in the previous month had interdicted 16,019 Haitians,[76] now also began to pick up hundreds of Cubans every day. In Florida, Lawton Chiles, now governor and facing a tough reelection battle, asked the federal government to declare an immigration emergency. When the administration declined to do so, Governor Chiles directed state agencies to prepare for an emergency "mass immigration," responding as they would for a hurricane.[77]

In Washington, President Clinton was caught in an ambiguous troika of interests: the imperatives of foreign policy, the sometimes conflicting demands of domestic pressure groups, and the desire to avoid enormous and continuing resettlement costs. Cuba was still a communist country, but it no longer represented a significant challenge internationally or within the region. The last remaining members of the Soviet military brigade that had been sent to Cuba after the missile crisis of 1962 had left the island the previous summer.[78] Refusing to accept large numbers of Cubans would keep the discontented in Cuba and might hasten Castro's downfall. It would also show Castro that he had not unnerved the administration.

The influence of pressure groups was more complicated. Clinton's political strategists, already preparing for the president's reelection in 1996, did not want to chance Governor Chiles' losing the governor's position. A gubernatorial loss in Florida in 1994 would complicate Clinton's chances

there in 1996. Florida, the fourth most populous state, with twenty-five elec-
toral votes, was a critical swing state; it could go to either the Democrats or the
Republicans. Blacks and anglos did not want another Mariel and might register
their displeasure at the voting booth. The Cuban-American community itself
was ambivalent about welcoming another mass escape, with its likely problems
and the backlash it would cause. Settled in Florida, they worried about the
inclusion of criminals among the newcomers, overcrowding in schools, shortages of housing, and costs to the taxpayers. "We have to take care of our city,"
commented Pedro Freyre, a lawyer who came to Miami in 1960. "We have
children here. We're beginning to see the fruits of our labor. There is definitely
a conflict of interest."[79] And although Cuban-Americans personally were willing to receive relatives and friends, abstractly they felt that keeping the disaffected in Cuba would hasten Castro's downfall. When balseros were few and it
was risky to flee Cuba, they were viewed as heroes. But when the numbers
rose and their departure was unimpeded, their heroic status diminished. CANF
shared this ambiguity. When Governor Chiles urged Washington to halt the
exodus, he was supported by CANF. CANF, however, was no longer the single
voice of the Cuban-American community. The Cuban-American community
was in transition, and so was its exile politics.

The exile establishment, represented by CANF, was being challenged by
new leaders, new groups, and new philosophies. Polls confirmed that many
Cuban-Americans, particularly younger adults and those who came in more
recent immigration waves, favored a variety of tactics to bring democracy to
Cuba.[80] Cubans who had left their homeland as youngsters had now assimilated into the United States. Their roots were not in Cuba, but in Florida, New
York, and New Jersey. These Cuban-Americans wanted a different version of
US-Cuban relations. Unlike CANF hardliners, whose goal is to remove Castro
from power, the new groups, such as the Cuban Committee for Democracy, the
Cuban American Defense League, Cambio Cuba, the Cuban-American Committee for Peace, and others, want to move the Cuban government toward
democracy. Some of these moderate groups believe that after more than three
and a half decades the hard-line position has not worked. They oppose the trade
embargo and other sanctions that impose hardships on the Cuban population.
They recognize that the aging Castro will not remain in power, and they want
to open a dialogue with the Cuban government.[81]

President Clinton, roiled by the competing pressures of the troika of
interests, on August 19, 1994, announced his first policy response to the
mass escape. In his opening statement at a news conference, he said:

> Today I have ordered that illegal refugees from Cuba will not be allowed to
> enter the United States. Refugees rescued at sea will be taken to our naval

base at Guantanamo while we explore the possibility of other safe havens within the region. . . . The United States will detain, investigate and, if necessary, prosecute Americans who take to the sea to pick up Cubans. Vessels used in such activities will be seized.[82]

Responding to a series of follow-up questions, the president stated that he supported the embargo and the Cuban Democracy Act and believed "we should not change our policy there." The Cuban Adjustment Act would continue to be "the law of the land," but "the Cubans who come here now . . . will not simply be released into the population. . . . We will review all their cases in light of the applicable law."[83]

Cubans, for the first time, had become "illegal refugees." Henceforth, they could enter the United States only through an in-country program in Cuba, having first applied for admission through the US Interests Section in Havana. Both Cubans and Haitians were now officially called "migrants in detention." Advocates had for years demanded that Haitians be given equity with Cubans; now Cubans were being given a perverse equity with Haitians.

The Clinton announcement abruptly reversed more than three decades of welcome for Cubans. Despite a barrage of radio announcements to that effect, Cubans refused to believe they would be denied entry to the United States and continued to leave the island. By September, there would be close to 32,000 Cubans in Guantanamo.[84] Shortly after announcing the new nonentry policy, Clinton instituted further measures to place economic and political pressure on Castro. Americans were prohibited from sending money to Cuba, and charter flights to the island were cut off. No longer would Cuban-Americans be allowed to make cash gifts to their families in Cuba. The general license granted for family visits, professional research, and news gathering was replaced by licenses granted by the Treasury Department. Specific licenses would be given for compelling humanitarian needs, such as a grave family illness, and to professional full-time journalists but not to freelance journalists. The number of US travelers to Cuba was cut by about 90 percent. The new policy, designed to hurt Castro, in effect hurt the Cuban people who depended on money from friends and relatives in the United States. At the same time, the new policy diminished access by the American public to information about Cuba.[85] Following these two major policy changes, the Clinton administration began intense negotiations with the Castro government.

After eight days of talks, on September 9, the United States and Cuba reached an agreement "to ensure that migration between the two countries is safe, legal, and orderly." The agreement settled two issues that had long been in contention. For years, Cuba had objected that the United States did not prosecute boat hijackers. (The United States had only begun prosecuting

hijackers of planes after an agreement was reached during the Carter administration.) In a sharp departure from previous practice, the United States
would no longer condone the hijacking of boats or planes. In return, the
Castro government agreed to discourage unsafe departures. A second area
of conflict had been the policy of the United States to encourage defections
from Cuba. The agreement stated, "Migrants rescued at sea attempting to
enter the United States will not be permitted to enter the United States, but
instead will be taken to safe haven facilities outside the United States."[86]
From those safe havens, Cubans would not be admitted directly to the
United States but would have to return to Cuba to apply for immigrant
visas. The State Department had long argued that Cubans must be admitted
to the United States because, under Cuban law, if they were returned, they
would be subject to prosecution for illegal departure. Cuba consented to
accept the "voluntary return" of Cubans from safe havens in Guantanamo
and Panama.

The accord, in addition to reducing the risks to escaping Cubans, removed the threat of a mass escape to the United States. However, the price
for these assurances was that no Cubans would be permitted to request
asylum. Any Cuban in need of asylum would have to apply for refugee
status from Cuba. The United States agreed to admit at least 20,000 Cubans
annually—immigrants, refugees, and parolees—directly from Cuba. In the
first year of the agreement, 26,700 would be admitted. (This was the first
time the United States agreed to establish a "floor"—committing itself to
admit a minimal number—rather than a ceiling.) The day after the agreement was announced, Cubans at Guantanamo rioted in protest against the
requirement that they return to Cuba to apply for admission to the United
States. Within days, Cuban police were arresting persons with rafts or materials to build rafts. Departures by sea stopped. The Cuban crisis of 1994 had
ended.[87]

Not only Cubans but many Americans felt that too high a price had been
paid to end the crisis. Frank Calzon, the Washington representative of Freedom House, spoke for human rights groups when he said: "It's almost as if
the West has asked Erich Honecker to stop Germans from crossing over the
Berlin Wall."[88] For years the United States had pressed for the right of free
exit, but that right vanished before the fear of mass escape to Florida and its
political consequences.

The domestic interests of the policy troika—satisfying various Cuban
pressure groups and allaying other groups' fears of huge resettlement
costs—had overridden important human rights issues: freedom of expression, freedom of movement, protection against indefinite detention, and the
right not to be forcibly repatriated. The new policies curbed the flow of

people and information between Cuba and the United States, restricting freedom of expression. The United States, in September 1992, ratified the International Covenant on Civil and Political Rights (ICCPR). Article 19 of the ICCPR protects the right to freedom of expression, which includes "freedom to seek, receive and impart information and ideas of all kinds, regardless of frontiers. . . . " The right of Americans to travel abroad and form their own judgments is critical to their ability to participate in public debate. The restriction on freelance journalists is particularly onerous.

The insistence by the United States that Castro prevent departures from Cuba violates Article 12 of the covenant which protects the right of everyone "to be free to leave any country, including his own." The Universal Declaration of Human Rights and the American Convention on Human Rights also guarantee the right of departure. Ironically, for years the United States championed the right to free emigration from the USSR, Soviet bloc countries, and Cuba. Political expediency has now dictated that that right be abandoned.

The United States' insistence on indefinitely detaining Cubans in "safe haven" camps until they return voluntarily to Cuba or are accepted for entry by a third country is tantamount to detention. Indefinite detention violates the ICCPR's Article 9. United States law "authorizes detention of undocumented people only pending inspection, exclusion or deportation, none of which apply to the Cuban detainees."[89] Repatriation to Cuba, human rights advocates argue, violates the Refugee Convention. Repatriation, even "voluntary" repatriation, to a dangerous situation is a form of refoulement. Rather, escapees should be screened for refugee status before they are returned to Cuba.[90]

The issue of repatriation to Cuba was heard almost immediately by a federal court. The plaintiffs contended that the administration was maintaining unbearable conditions at the Guantanamo safe haven in order that the detainees would request "voluntary" repatriation. Their class action suit asked that the repatriation be stopped and that lawyers be given access to the detainees. At the end of October, Judge C. Clyde Atkins ruled that no repatriations, even voluntary ones, could take place until the detainees were allowed to see lawyers. Because Guantanamo was United States territory, the detainees were entitled to due process under the First Amendment.[91] Within days, a federal appeals court set aside Judge Atkins' ruling. In January 1995, a three-judge panel of the Eleventh Circuit Court of Appeals handed down two important decisions, *Cuban American Bar Association (CABA) v. Christopher* and *Haitian Refugee Center (HRC) v. Christopher,* which are likely to remain established law.[92]

In the CABA case the court ruled that migrants in safe havens outside the United States do not have the constitutional rights of due process and equal protection and are not protected against forced return by the UN Refugee Convention or the Immigration and Naturalization Act. In the HRC case the court stated that the "control and jurisdiction" that the United States exercised in Guantanamo were not equivalent to sovereignty. Refugee authority Bill Frelick summed up the implications of these cases:

> The prospect looms that the US government will convert Guantanamo into a permanent refugee holding facility, not limited to Haitians and Cubans nor reserved specifically for mass refugee emergencies. Guantanamo, and perhaps the Panama Canal Zone and other foreign military bases as well, could potentially be used to keep individuals representing a wide spectrum of nationalities from seeking asylum inside the United States, thus denying them access to due process rights and allowing them to be repatriated forcibly whenever the United States deems it in its own interests to return them.[93]

Although the courts were upholding the government's position, even before the CABA and HRC cases were decided Cubans were being released from detention. Softening his position somewhat, in October President Clinton announced that parole would be granted to those over seventy, unaccompanied minors, and those with serious medical conditions and their caregivers. Early in December, Attorney General Janet Reno announced that on a case-by-case basis she would consider for parole Cuban children and their families who would suffer extraordinary hardship if they had to remain for a long time in safe havens in Guantanamo and Panama. However, only families with "full financial sponsorship in the United States" would be eligible for parole. These four categories became known as the four protocols.[94] Despite the relaxation of the rules, over 20,000 Cubans remained locked up in Guantanamo. With the prospect of indefinite detention and rioting, in May 1995 the Clinton administration announced a new and very different policy.

The new policy was the product of a review by three top Clinton confidantes, Samuel R. Berger, Morton H. Halperin, and Peter Tarnoff. The only outsiders the three consulted—in order to gauge the domestic political consequences—were Florida's Senator Bob Graham and Governor Lawton Chiles. The State Department's coordinator of Cuban affairs and Jorge Mas Canosa, the chairman of CANF, were deliberately excluded. Tarnoff met secretly with Ricardo Alarcón, Castro's confidant who heads Cuba's Parliament, and together they came to an accord.

The accord was a double reversal of previous policy. All the Cubans at Guantanamo (save those with criminal histories) who previously had been denied entry would be admitted to the United States. And, in an even more stunning reversal, Cubans picked up at sea would not all be taken to a safe haven. Rather, they would be interviewed briefly; those who were not found to have a "genuine need for protection" would be returned to Cuba. In Cuba they could apply for refugee status through the US Interests Section in Havana.[95]

Repercussions were immediate. While applauding the admission of the Guantanamo Cubans, most Cuban-Americans were unhappy that escapees would be returned to Cuba. Hardliners feared the new agreement might presage a rapprochement with Havana. In the House of Representatives and the Senate, Republicans pushed bills—opposed by the Clinton administration—to strengthen the trade embargo.[96] Human rights advocates were unhappy about the interdiction and the process for evaluating refugee claims on board ship.[97]

In a further reversal of policy, in October 1995, Clinton signed an executive order that eased restrictions on travel and sending money to Cuba. The order called for an easing of travel restrictions for Cuban-Americans who want to visit Cuba, academics, artists, and members of the clergy. Cuban-Americans could send up to $300 every three months to relatives who suffered from disasters such as fire or storms. In other attempts at improving communications between Cuba and the United States, Clinton allowed American and Cuban undergraduates to study in each other's countries and American news organizations to open bureaus in Cuba.[98]

The easing of restrictions on travel, money, and news gathering was a prelude to the closing of Guantanamo as a safe haven. In November of 1995 the last Haitians were returned home; at the end of January 1996, the last Cubans were flown to Florida. The government officially closed down the tent cities that had housed thousands of Haitians and Cubans.[99] The mass escapes of the summer of 1994 have withered away. As had all previous administrations, the Clinton administration had responded in an ad hoc fashion to the troika of interests.

Refugee policy, trampled by the troika of interests, has been progressively debased in order to achieve control of our borders and to extend them offshore. Restrictions on the right to depart, requiring refugees to apply for resettlement from within their own countries, interdicting and repatriating escapees, denying asylum seekers due process, and confining them to indefinite detention are not principles that accord with respect for human rights. The United States cannot possibly welcome all who have valid claims to refugee status. And certainly the forces that create refugee problems are not going to vanish. Yet it is possible for the United States, working with the United Nations and regional organizations, to chart a new, humane, and viable refugee protection system.

7
Charting a New Course

In the more than three decades since the signing of the Protocol relating to the Status of Refugees, a single principle has remained paramount, the principle that any individual who fears persecution has the right to seek asylum in a foreign country. All the battles over the Haitian and Cuban and Central American refugees have been over that central principle—the right to seek asylum. In principle upheld, in practice the right to seek asylum has been circumvented, ignored, even abrogated.

The United Nations Convention relating to the Status of Refugees, adopted in 1951, for the first time defined precisely the grounds on which an individual could be considered a political refugee. More important, signatories to the convention and protocol, among them the United States in 1967, agreed not to return any individual who met those standards to the country in which he or she has a "well-founded fear of persecution." Groundbreaking in its time, the convention anticipated neither the wider grounds that today force individuals into flight nor the resistance of many signatories to meet their obligations fully.

While the Refugee Convention recognizes the right of the individual to *request* asylum and, further, not to be returned to potential persecution, the convention does not, indeed cannot, require any country to *grant* that asylum, or even to afford any standard of protection whatsoever. In other words, while individuals with a well-founded fear of persecution may flee their own countries, they may, and increasingly do, find all other doors closed to them.

President Ronald Reagan's lips spoke eloquently of the principles of the convention, but his hand signed an agreement with a Haitian dictator to interdict and return Haitian boat people. He extolled America as a land of freedom but excoriated the Central Americans who asked for freedom. Presidents George Bush and Bill Clinton countermanded the very bases for international refugee law, that a refugee has the right to flee a country in which he or she fears persecution, and that that same refugee has the right to seek asylum.

When first enacted in 1980, United States refugee law was grounded in humanitarian concern. The realities of government, however, balanced that concern against the demands of foreign policy and domestic pressures. Very quickly, foreign policy and domestic pressures became the major determinants of refugee policy, eclipsing humanitarian concern. In Central America, foreign policy dictated the eradication of Marxism. This meant that the United States supported repressive but right-wing governments, even training the forces that massacred, tortured, and intimidated. The easily foreseen result was that hundreds of thousands of people fled. But the foreign policy that helped to create the refugees then disclaimed that they were refugees. Denied legal entrance, the Central Americans, by the hundreds of thousands, entered illegally. Backlash was inevitable.

With the demise of the Soviet Union, the dominance of foreign policy in refugee policy gave way to domestic pressures to "control illegal immigration." At present, with foreign policy an unreliable guide, the will to restrict and restrain immigration has taken the reins, controlling the troika of interests that determine United States refugee policy. The American public demands that the numbers of both immigrants and refugees be reduced; the Congress accedes to those demands. But while the United States—and other refugee-receiving countries as well—closes its gates, all over the world there are exploding numbers not only of refugees but of others needing protection, including the internally displaced.

There need not be this conflict between admission and restriction, between the claims made by refugees and the claims made by citizens. By changing the course of its refugee policies and programs, the United States could far better respond to both, striking a long overdue balance between advocates for and opponents of refugees.

For the past half century, there have been three "durable solutions" to the problem of refugees: repatriation to the country of origin, settlement in a country of first asylum, or resettlement in a third country. These solutions alone will not now serve more than a tiny fraction of the world's refugees. Repatriation, the most desirable solution of all, cannot occur until the cause of the refugee flight has been resolved. Nor can refugees long remain in countries of first asylum, the majority of which are themselves often troubled by poverty and domestic conflict and unable or unwilling to give permanent refuge. Permanent resettlement, which the United States has traditionally offered, is given worldwide to about one of every hundred refugees. That proportion will certainly drop.[1]

The accepted "solutions" to the problem of refugees may, in fact, have exacerbated the underlying problems. The UN High Commissioner for Refugees, in its 1995 report, acknowledged that:

There is now a growing recognition that the world's response to refugee movements in the 1970s and 1980s may have actually contributed to the scale of the problem in the 1990s. The large-scale resettlement program for the Vietnamese boat people, for example, and the long-term assistance programmes provided to many refugees in Africa, continue to obstruct the search for solutions in those parts of the world.

At the same time, new population displacements are taking place for which none of the traditional solutions seem to be appropriate. . . . And what kind of solutions will be available for the growing numbers of people displaced within their own country? Will they eventually be able to return to the communities they left, or will alternative solutions have to be devised?[2]

Moreover, resettlement and assistance were given to those who fled civil disorder, but there was no aid for those who remained.

If we can acknowledge that the traditional solutions are no longer the only, or even the best solutions, then we can begin to look in new directions to search for alternative, and possibly better, paths of action. Perhaps the critical change here is the change from solution to search. Law professor David Martin sees "some unintended benefits . . . possible as an outgrowth of the new public resistance and anxiety." He feels that the resistance of the public to refugees and asylum seekers "could force the serious consideration of novel responses to the threats and needs that uproot people from their homes."[3]

But as we consider new responses to the needs of refugees, two things must be kept in mind. First, that the old solutions do not have to be abandoned; first asylum, resettlement, and repatriation remain sometimes viable ways to assist refugees. Second, and more important, we must stop thinking primarily of "solutions." The problem of the world's refugees is infinitely complex; refugees cannot be helped if we grasp at simple answers. Rather, we must think of a progression of options. That progression should begin even before any refugee has been forced to flee his or her country.

The UNHCR now recognizes that alongside the right to leave one's country, there are also the "right to remain" and the "right not to be displaced."[4] Increasingly, therefore, attention is turning to the prevention of refugee flows. Prevention, however, must not be confused with preemption. The United States prevented a refugee flow from Haiti by confining fleeing Haitians to their island. When, in 1991, Iraqis began to flee to Turkey, a safe haven zone was created within Iraq because, it was feared, mass movements of refugees would "threaten international peace and security in the region."[5] Similarly, safe haven zones were created in Bosnia, in order to "avert new flows of refugees and displaced persons from Bosnia and Hercegovina."[6] In each of these refugee crises, action was taken initially not to protect the refugees, but to protect neighboring countries from the refugees.

When we speak of prevention, we do not mean preventing refugee movements, but rather preventing the abuses that cause those refugee movements. And just as refugees are driven by a mingling of political and economic impetuses, so must both roots be addressed if refugee movements are to be prevented. To offer economic assistance while condoning political repression is irresponsible. To urge political reform while there is economic scarcity is callous. The United States followed the former course in Haiti, the latter in Cuba. Haiti had been economically and socially desiccated by decades of kleptocratic government, yet the United States continued to pour aid into the country, much of which never percolated below the wealthy ruling class. The United States followed the opposite course in Cuba, condemning Castro's repressive government, while strangling the economy on which the Cuban people depended.

In Central America, the pressure for economic and social reform found political expression. The United States saw only the political expression and ignored the need for economic and social reform. The Nicaraguan government was Marxist, and so were the Salvadoran rebels; both had to be defeated. In El Salvador, therefore, the United States assisted the oligarchy and its strongarm military; in Nicaragua, we fomented armed opposition to the government. In both cases, the result was a cruel and protracted civil war that brought no relief of deeper social and economic problems.

Sadako Ogata, the UN High Commissioner for Refugees, observed a "strong and indisputable relationship" between lack of development and internal conflict and the generation of displaced persons and refugees.[7] This assertion is supported by comparing UNHCR's data on refugee movements with the UN's Human Development Index (HDI), a ranking of states according to income, life expectancy, and educational level. Not surprisingly, "countries with the highest ranking on the HDI are the least likely to experience mass population displacements." None of the thirty countries ranked highest on the scale produced refugees. No more surprisingly, the lowest thirty countries generated large-scale refugee movements. But it cannot be argued that poverty alone engenders refugee movements. Many countries ranked low on the scale, such as Tanzania, Nepal, Malawi, and Guinea, were giving refuge, not creating refugees.[8] Even extreme deprivation, as in Bolivia or Burkina Faso, does not drive people from their homes.[9]

It is not poverty alone but the presence of poverty together with the denial of human rights that causes large-scale refugee displacements. Human rights and economic development must be linked. If, for example, the United States offers economic aid, it should be directed not just to economic production, but also to such areas as education and health care.

But as a condition of economic aid, we must also demand the advancement of, for example, the right to free speech or the right to organize. And if we demand reform, we must go one step further and stop training and supplying the armies or paramilitary forces that carry out a government's repression. These demands will carry greater weight if they are made not just by the United States, but by the United States acting in concert with other nations in the region.

Madame Ogata has said that "today's refugee problems cannot be treated in isolation from the political, social and economic causes which give rise to them."[10] Thus, if we are to prevent refugee flows, we must first attempt to ameliorate their causes. Gil Loescher, an expert on refugees and the international refugee regime, has advised, "The global refuge problem is not a humanitarian problem requiring charity but is a political problem requiring political solutions, and as such it cannot be separated from other areas of international concern such as migration, human rights, international security and development assistance."[11]

Prevention of abuses may involve early identification of the problem, diplomatic intervention, and, in the most extraordinary circumstances, humanitarian intervention. The Commission on Global Governance has observed, "Recent history shows that extreme circumstances can arise within countries when the security of people is so extensively imperiled that external collective action under international law becomes justified."[12] Humanitarian intervention, sanctioned by the UN or a regional organization, can protect a country's citizens against the most blatant violations of human rights.

It would be utopian to envision that every refugee flow could be prevented. Many arise from ethnic, social, and political conflicts so deep that they find redress only in civil war. Such was the case in El Salvador. Refugees from civil war, unless they live in border areas, do not immediately travel to another country. In general, they first move to safe areas within their own country. The UN convention defines a refugee as someone who is "*outside* the country of his nationality" (emphasis added). Neither the convention nor the US Refugee Act provides for the protection of the internally displaced, refugees who remain within their countries. Moreover, the grounds on which one can claim refugee status are precisely defined: A refugee is a person who has "a well-founded fear of being persecuted for reasons of race, religion, nationality, membership of a particular social group or political opinion." This definition is fitting for individuals in need of resettlement; it may not always be fitting for groups of people in need of protection.

Two regional instruments have devised broader definitions of who is a refugee. The Organization of African Unity, in 1969, agreed to a convention that adds to the UN definition the following:

> The term "refugee" shall also apply to every person who, owing to external aggression, occupation, foreign domination or events seriously disturbing public order in either part or the whole of his country of origin or nationality, is compelled to leave his place of habitual residence in order to seek refuge in another place outside his country of origin or nationality.[13]

The Cartagena Declaration on Refugees, signed in 1984 by ten nations in Latin America, also broadens the refugee definition; it:

> includes among refugees persons who have fled their country because their lives, safety or freedom have been threatened by generalized violence, foreign aggression, internal conflicts, massive violation of human rights or other circumstances which have seriously disturbed the public order.[14]

Both instruments have defined more generously who is a refugee. At the same time, neither has extended that definition to those who remain within their own countries. It would be unwise for the United States to broaden its definition of a refugee. To do so would mean that every refugee from foreign invasion, civil war, or martial law would have grounds to seek asylum or refugee status. The United Nations definition should continue to be the US standard for the granting of refugee status or asylum. However, the Cartagena definition should be the US standard for providing protection. Such protection might be needed within a country, as in safe zones; outside the country, in regional safe havens; or within the United States, under temporary protected status.

Arthur Helton, of the Open Society Institute, has advocated that the United States, along with other countries in the hemisphere, enter into a compact for the protection and assistance of refugees. The signatories would receive the refugees, transport them to a safe haven, and guarantee their protection, "complying with internationally-recognized standards for fundamental human rights, including the principle of *non-refoulement,* and the prohibition on rejecting asylum seekers at national borders."[15]

Law professor Harold Hongju Koh has detailed how such protection could have been offered to Haitians. He writes:

> The Clinton administration could have asked the United Nations and/or the OAS to establish safe-haven zones at several sites inside Haiti. Such zones could have been established near the islands and coast cities known to be prime departure points for boat people seeking to flee Haiti. . . . These safe-haven zones could have been controlled or monitored by UNHCR, and pro-

tected by a multinational OAS or UN peacekeeping force, to provide refugees with food, shelter, and protection from persecution. Such zones would have provided refugees temporary safe haven inside Haiti, thereby controlling migration consistent with American interests by reducing Haitians' incentive to take to the high seas. An international presence within Haiti would have further exerted pressure on the Haitian military junta to comply with international minimum standards. Moreover, overseas refugee processing could have taken place within the safe-haven zones in Haiti, overseen by international human rights monitors from both UNHCR and nongovernmental organizations.[16]

Protection may also be necessary when peace is being restored and refugees are returning to their homes. International protection was extended in Haiti after Jean-Bertrand Aristide was restored to the presidency and after René Préval was freely elected Aristide's successor. Returning refugees may also remain in need of protection.[17] In 1995, more than twelve years after being forced from their villages by the military, thousands of Guatemalan Indians began returning home from Mexico. But they were not yet safe: The Guatemalan army attacked a refugee settlement in the Xalbal region, killing a dozen people and wounding more than two dozen. The refugees continued to be caught in crossfire between the army and the guerrillas.

Just as humanitarian prevention does not guarantee that there will be no refugee flows, protection does not assure that all internally displaced people and refugees will find safety. As we have said, in order to assist refugees, we must offer a progression of options. Some refugees who do not find protection in their own countries, or in areas of safe haven, will travel farther in search of safety. Still others need the permanent resettlement offered only by asylum.

Among the hundreds of thousands who left Cuba, Haiti, and Central America, there were many who had a well-founded fear of persecution. For them, flight and a request for asylum were the only alternatives to persecution or death. When asylum seekers come individually, or in small groups, their claims can be heard and decided fairly and speedily. But in a seeming tidal wave of mass escape, these asylum seekers become indistinguishable from others who fear generalized violence or civil disorder and those who come to reunite with families or improve their standard of living. The public demands that the floodgates be closed. Policy makers comply. All—the genuine refugees and the would-be immigrants—are shut out.

There is a further complication. Prescreening can identify those refugees who may have a well-founded fear of persecution; they can be admitted to the United States and ask for asylum. The same prescreening can also identify those who come only to reunite with family or to improve their standard of living; they can be deported. But, particularly when people are fleeing civil war or a breakdown of the political order, there will be large numbers of people who cannot be admitted because they cannot meet the refugee standard, but should not be deported because they are in need of protection. In the first such crisis of mass escape, the Mariel boatlift, all three categories were eventually admitted, under a special entrant status. When, soon after, the Salvadorans and, in lesser numbers, the Guatemalans began coming, the government, fearing another Mariel, resolved that all should be deported. But their numbers were far too great for even the most resolute efforts to exclude them. In the end, the Salvadorans had to be given temporary protected status. When the status expires, those who have not qualified for asylum will be required to leave unless this status is extended. With the mass escapes of Cubans and Haitians in the summer of 1994, the most draconian actions were taken: to permit no one even to apply for asylum in the United States.

A far more humane policy was put in place when for a time Haitians and Cubans were taken to Guantanamo for protection and screening. Rather than foreclosing this option, we should have maintained it. Moreover, the safe haven that was provided at Guantanamo could become a model for future mass escapes, whether by sea or over land. Placing escapees in protection should be the standard procedure whenever the numbers of asylum seekers arriving in a short period of time become so great that they threaten to overwhelm the system. Several purposes would be served by transferring escapees to a safe haven. First, no person with a well-founded fear of persecution would be subjected to refoulement. Second, the corps of asylum officers could screen and adjudicate applications free of public pressure. Third, all the escapees, even those who did not meet the stringent standard of the Refugee Convention, would be protected. And finally, when screening had been completed, the third group, those who were entitled to neither asylum nor protection, could be returned home.

Brunson McKinley, an official in the State Department, argued that in a safe haven even prescreening would not be necessary. In a safe haven, he said, "You accept all comers, you do not question their motives, you feed and protect them, but don't let them come to the United States. In other words, you create a mechanism in which the boat people themselves are encouraged to decide whether the need for protection or the desire to immigrate is the primary motivation."[18] Even if one does not accept McKinley's position that no one be permitted to come to the United States, the United States has still met its obligations, to the law and to the refugees, by providing the refugees with first asylum.

Along the same pragmatic lines of thinking, if there is no flood of refugees across American borders, there will be no public backlash. It is less the fear of newcomers than the fear of numbers that agitates the American public. If, as is likely, the United States must accept some of the refugees for admission, their resettlement can be carried out in an orderly and compassionate way. And each uneventful resettlement makes the next resettlement easier.

The desire to regularize refugee admissions lies behind in-country processing programs. These programs ask that those who seek refuge in the United States apply for that status within their own countries, then await approval. The Haitian in-country processing program was seriously flawed. It was unavailable to many who needed it. Its staffing and procedures were inadequate. And it failed to protect the few who came under its aegis. In-country processing in Cuba, prior to the summer of 1994, granted few entry visas. After the September 1994 migration agreement between the United States and Cuba, the number granted entry rose dramatically. But in-country processing in Cuba, like the programs in Vietnam and Russia, has become an orderly departure immigration program, rather than protection for persons fleeing persecution.

The term "in-country processing of refugees" is an oxymoron. Immigrants apply for visas before leaving their countries; if they are denied immigration visas, they return to their homes with no fear of reprisal. Refugees, on the other hand, are by definition outside their countries. If they are not, then it is the danger they face there that sends them in search of asylum. Yet in-country processing requires that refugees remain in their country, that they come to a public office, such as the US embassy, to apply for asylum, then return to their homes (often for several months) and await approval. The very act of applying for asylum brands these people as dissidents and only adds to their risk of persecution. Moreover, if they have been in hiding, they must appear publicly first to apply and then, since they have no regular address, to inquire about their status.

Yet, in fiscal year 1994, nearly 80 percent of the refugees admitted to the United States came through in-country processing.[19] Such programs, which in 1995 existed in Vietnam, the former Soviet Union, and Cuba, in the words of Kathleen Newland "give higher priority to order than to urgency in removing people from a situation in which they have good reason to fear persecution. . . . The most compelling refugee cases are the least likely to be able to use these programs."[20] At best, in-country processing can benefit two classes of people: those, such as former political prisoners, whom the government no longer wishes to punish, or others who are the focus of international attention and are therefore somewhat safe from reprisal. For most others the risks of applying for asylum in-country are far greater than the risks of flight. Most at risk is the very concept of refugee protection.

Refugee protection and orderly departure need not be mutually exclusive. If safe havens are established, they could also serve, as Professor Koh has suggested, as the bases for orderly departure programs. The needs of both the United States and the refugees would be served. The refugees' "departure" would be less hazardous, while the United States could determine their claims to asylum in an "orderly" manner. Those denied resettlement would still be entitled to the protection afforded by a safe haven.

People seeking asylum in the United States must come here to request it. For many of these people, that request is made at a port of entry; others will cross the border before they ask for asylum. Along its borders, the United States, however, is strengthening enforcement, making them less vulnerable to entrance by the undocumented. Sections of the border have been literally walled off; the INS has increased the number of its Border Patrol agents; even the armed forces have been enlisted for support.[21] All of these efforts aim to intercept undocumented persons before they enter the United States. But among those persons may be refugees, who frequently have no documentation. United States immigration law is complex: It requires that people entering the United States have documents permitting them to do so; but it also allows asylum seekers to enter without such documents.

The Border Patrol is an enforcement arm of the immigration service. What it enforces, however, is the barring of the undocumented; the Border Patrol has been given neither training nor incentive to assist asylum seekers. Its enforcement role is not compatible with a protection role. Along the southern border, its mission is to prevent undocumented Mexicans, and others, from entering the United States. But a person's nationality does not reveal his or her motivations. Late in 1995, the United States granted political asylum to fifty-five Mexicans,[22] illustrating the complexity of the situation. Moreover, Border Patrol agents wear uniforms and carry guns; refugees fleeing from military forces are unlikely to ask them for legal refugee protection.

The Border Patrol has been given the task of enforcement. The task of protection must be given to others. There ought to be independent observers working alongside the Border Patrol whose role it is to ascertain whether among those attempting to enter the country there are refugees who should be permitted to request asylum. These observers could be a part of and receive training with the corps of asylum adjudicators. (Legislation was introduced by the Clinton administration during the 103d Congress to mandate such officers at the border. The legislation has not yet been acted on.[23]) Their task would be to guard against the refoulement, the forcible return, of genuine refugees. The two arms—enforcement and protection—working together would ensure that United States immigration law was carried out wholly. The undocumented with no claim to protection would be deported; those in need of asylum would have their claims adjudicated. More than a legal obligation, the right to ask asylum remains a necessary step along the ,progression, the step that follows humanitarian prevention and the provision of safe haven and temporary protection.

A provision of safe haven can also obtain in the United States. The standard for granting asylum is a narrow one; in the United States, in 1995, slightly more than 20 percent of applicants were successful. Yet there are others who, though they do not qualify for asylum, are not, for humanitarian reasons, deported. Although the Western European countries gave asylum to only one of ten applicants, an additional three who were unable to return to countries in conflict were permitted to remain under what is commonly known as "humanitarian status."[24] The United States now has enacted a temporary protected status. This status could be used to protect not only national groups but individuals. If an individual's asylum claim is denied, but the person comes from an area in conflict, she could be registered for temporary protected status. The status would be revoked when it is once again safe for her to return home.

The protection of refugees is both a progression and continuous. It is a progression that begins with preventing the abuses that propel refugees and ends only when the refugee has found stability and safety. Refugee protection is also continuous: There is no certain prevention of refugee flows, nor is there any certain solution for the refugees themselves. It would be short-sighted to assume that measures taken early in the progression will avert the need for later measures. Early intervention does not always succeed; refugee protection may fail or may go on for so long that more permanent solutions are called for. Conversely, even years after refugees have been resettled, changes in their home countries may persuade some of them to return. But there is one constant in the progression—the idea of safe haven. At every stage of the progression, the goal is to enable people, whether in their home countries or abroad, to live in safety.

The year 1980 was pivotal in American refugee history. In that year, the United States enacted its first comprehensive refugee legislation. In many ways, the Refugee Act of 1980 was looking backward; it put into force a protocol that had been signed in 1967. Its attention was focused primarily on refugees, and to a lesser degree on asylees, limiting its vision to those who would be permanently resettled in the United States. It also assumed that the United States would act primarily as a third country, for the most part accepting refugees for resettlement in an ordered and selective manner.

Within six weeks of the passage of the act, the future had been thrust upon it. The refugees who arrived from the Caribbean and, shortly thereafter, from Central America did not necessarily meet the definition of the postwar convention and protocol. They did not come to the United States from a country of first asylum; the United States was that country. They had not been screened, selected, or processed as refugees in third countries applying to resettle in the United States.

Much of United States refugee policy in the years since has been an attempt to return to the status quo ante. When it has failed, as with the attempt to deny due process of law to Salvadorans, the failure engendered chaos. When it has succeeded, as in refusing entry to Haitian asylum seekers, the success has come at the expense of law and conscience. Looking backward has only allowed us to turn away from the problems. We need now to look forward and squarely address the problems.

Carl Kaysen, a professor of political economy, has written:

> Fundamental solutions to the refugee problem require either permanent reset- tlement or repatriation. At a deeper level, they depend on prevention: the avoidance of the kind of violent civil conflict and government repression and persecution of its citizens that generate the refugee flow. . . . Repatriation and prevention require similar and similarly difficult conditions: for the first, the creation of civil peace and the end of repression and persecution by govern- ments of some or all their citizens; for the second, the maintenance of those conditions: civil peace and reasonably liberal governments respectful of the human rights of all their citizens. This is a tall order. A tall order, but not impossible.[25]

The United States, together with other countries, must direct its best efforts not to preventing refugee flows but to preventing the abuses that give rise to refugees. Not every civil war can be ended, but some can. Not every repressive government can be reformed, but some can. Not every refugee flow can be stemmed, but refugees can be assisted. To some we can offer safe haven. And finally, in the words of Atle Grahl-Madsen: "When every other safeguard fails, asylum in a foreign country becomes the ulti- mate human right."[26]

If we respond to the needs of refugees as a progression of options, rather than as opposing options of resettlement or return, we will respond better to the refugees and better also to the American people.

Endnotes

Notes for Introduction

1. *New York Times,* June 20, 1995, p. 4.
2. James F. Hollifield, "Immigration and Republicanism in France: The Hidden Consensus," in Wayne A. Cornelius, Philip L. Martin, and James F. Hollifield, eds., *Controlling Immigration: A Global Perspective* (Stanford, CA: Stanford University Press, 1992), p. 171.
3. 8 CFR 208.14(e).

Notes for Chapter 1

1. Barbara Jordan, "The Americanization Ideal," *New York Times,* September 11, 1995, p. 15.
2. Buchanan, quoted in Bill Frelick, "Haitian Boat Interdiction and Return: First Asylum and First Principles of Refugee Protection," *Cornell International Law Journal,* Vol. 26 (1993), p. 680.
3. "Text of Reagan's Speech Accepting the Republican Nomination," *New York Times,* July 18, 1980, p. 8.
4. William S. Bernard, "A History of US Immigration Policy," in Richard A. Easterlin, David Ward, William S. Bernard, and Reed Ueda, eds., *Immigration* (Cambridge, MA: Harvard University Press, 1982), p. 76.
5. Elizabeth Hull, *Without Justice for All: The Constitutional Rights of Aliens* (Westport, CT: Greenwood Press, 1985), p. 9.
6. Robert A. Pastor, "Caribbean Emigration and US Immigration Policy: Cross Currents," paper, Conference on International Relations of the Contemporary Caribbean, Inter-American University of Puertò Rico, April 22–23, 1983, p. 7.
7. Hull, *Without Justice for All,* p. 9.
8. Hull, *Without Justice for All,* p. 11.
9. Edward A. Steiner, *The Immigrant Tide, Its Ebb and Flow* (New York: Fleming H. Revell, 1909), p. 17.
10. E.P. Hutchinson, *Legislative History of American Immigration Polciy: 1798–1965* (Philadelphia: University of Pennsylvania Press, 1981), pp. 127–28.
11. Robert A. Divine, *American Immigration Policy, 1924–1952* (New Haven, CT: Yale University Press, 1957), p. 4.
12. Hull, *Without Justice for All,* p. 163.
13. *The Crisis,* Vol. 9, No. 4 (February 1915), p. 190.
14. Divine, *American Immigration Policy,* pp. 11–13.
15. *New York Times,* August 20, 1995, p. 1; Arthur S. Link, *American Epoch: A History of the United States Since the 1890's* (New York: Alfred A. Knopf, 1956), p. 17.
16. Bernard, "A History of US Immigration Policy," p. 97.
17. Dennis Gallagher, *The Evolution of the International Refugee System* (Washington, DC: Refugee Policy Group, June 1988), p. 8.

18. Alan Dowty, *Closed Borders: The Contemporary Assault on Freedom of Movement* (New Haven, CT: Yale University Press, 1987), p. 89.

19. W.R. Smyser, *Refugees: Extended Exile* (New York: Praeger Publishers, 1987), pp. 6–7; Aristide R. Zolberg, Astri Suhrke, and Sergio Aguayo, *Escape from Violence: Conflict and the Refugee Crisis in the Developing World* (New York: Oxford University Press, 1989), pp. 19–20.

20. Dowty, *Closed Borders*, p. 91.

21. Dowty, *Closed Borders*, p. 92.

22. Divine, *American Immigration Policy*, p. 48.

23. Norman L. Zucker and Naomi Flink Zucker, *The Guarded Gate: The Reality of American Refugee Policy* (San Diego, CA: Harcourt Brace Jovanovich, 1987), pp. 20–21.

24. Henry L. Feingold, *The Politics of Rescue: The Roosevelt Administration and the Holocaust, 1938–1945* (New Brunswick, NJ: Rutgers University Press, 1970), p. 149.

25. Gordon Thomas and Max Morgan Witts, *Voyage of the Damned* (New York: Stein and Day, 1974), p. 252.

26. David S. Wyman, *Paper Walls: America and the Refugee Crisis 1938–1945* (Amherst, MA: University of Massachusetts Press, 1968), p. 173.

27. David S. Wyman, *The Abandonment of the Jews: America and the Holocaust, 1941–1945* (New York: Pantheon Books, 1984), p. 127.

28. Zucker and Zucker, *The Guarded Gate*, pp. 25–26.

29. Saul S. Friedman, *No Haven for the Oppressed: United States Policy toward Jewish Refugees, 1938–1945* (Detroit: Wayne State University Press, 1973), p. 218.

Notes for Chapter 2

1. Gil Loescher and John A. Scanlan, *Calculated Kindness: Refugees and America's Half-Open Door, 1945 to the Present* (New York: Free Press, 1986), p. 6.

2. Loescher and Scanlan, *Calculated Kindness*, p. 9.

3. Loescher and Scanlan, *Calculated Kindness*, p. 21.

4. Alan Trei, letter, *New York Times*, August 31, 1994, p. 18.

5. UNHCR, *The State of the World's Refugees 1993: The Challenge of Protection* (New York: Penguin Books, 1993), p. 11.

6. Dennis Gallagher, *The Evolution of the International Refugee System* (Washington, DC: Refugee Policy Group, June 1988), p. 23.

7. 1951 UN Convention relating to the Status of refugees.

8. 1951 UN Convention relating to the Status of refugees.

9. William S. Bernard, "A History of US Immigration Policy," in Richard A. Easterlin, David Ward, William S. Bernard, and Reed Ueda, eds., *Immigration* (Cambridge, MA: Harvard University Press, 1982), p. 102.

10. James L. Carlin, *The Refugee Connection: A Lifetime of Running a Lifeline* (London: Macmillan Press, 1989), p. 61.

11. Julia Vadala Taft, David S. North, and David A. Ford, *Refugee Resettlement in the US: Time for a New Focus* (Washington, DC: New TransCentury Foundation, 1979), p. 62.

12. Félix Roberto Masud-Piloto, *With Open Arms: Cuban Migration to the United States* (Totowa, NJ: Rowman and Littlefield, 1988), p. 21.

13. Gillian Gunn, *Cuba in Transition: Options for US Policy* (New York: Pantheon Books, 1988), p. 106.

14. George Black, *The Good Neighbor: How the United States Wrote the History of Central America and the Caribbean* (New York: Pantheon Books, 1988), p. 106.

15. Norman L. Zucker, "Refugee Resettlement in the United States: Policy and Problems," in Gilburt D. Loescher and John A. Scanlan, eds., *The Global Refugee Problem: US and World Response, The Annals of the American Academy of Political and Social Science,* Vol. 467 (May 1983, p. 174).

16. Robert L. Bach, "Cubans," in David W. Haines, ed., *Refugees in the United States: A Reference Handbook* (Westport, CT: Greenwood Press, 1985), p. 83; Norman L. Zucker and Naomi Flink Zucker, *The Guarded Gate: The Reality of American Refugee Policy* (San Diego, CA: Harcourt Brace Jovanovich, 1987), p. 33.

17. Alan Dowty, *Closed Borders: The Contemporary Assault on Freedom of Movement* (New Haven, CT: Yale University Press, 1987), p. 177.

18. Masud-Piloto, *With Open Arms,* p. 58.

19. Masud-Piloto, *With Open Arms,* p. 57.

20. Masud-Piloto, *With Open Arms,* p. 62.

21. Masud-Piloto, *With Open Arms,* pp. 62–63.

22. Bach, "Cubans," pp. 83–84; Zucker and Zucker, *The Guarded Gate,* p. 38.

23. Masud-Piloto, *With Open Arms,* p. 68.

24. Leo Cherne, "Economic Migrants," *New York Times,* October 3, 1981, p. 27.

25. Zucker and Zucker, *The Guarded Gate,* p. 180.

26. Frederick J. Conway and Susan Huelsebusch Buchanan, "Haitians," in Haines, *Refugees,* pp. 101–2.

27. *New York Times,* December 13, 1972, p. 4; letter signed by US Representatives Bella Abzug, Charles Rangel, and eight others, *New York Times,* August 23, 1973, p. 36.

28. Zucker and Zucker, *The Guarded Gate,* pp. 39–44.

29. *Refugee Reports,* Vol. 15, No. 12 (December 31, 1994), pp. 9–11.

30. Zucker and Zucker, *The Guarded Gate,* pp. 42–43.

31. Zucker and Zucker, *The Guarded Gate,* pp. 42–43.

32. *Refugee Reports,* Vol. 15, No. 12 (December 31, 1994), pp. 9–11; *New York Times,* September 9, 1987, p. 7.

33. *New York Times,* March 6, 1988, p. 3.

34. *New York Times,* July 9, 1988, p. 1.

35. Norman L. Zucker and Naomi Flink Zucker, "The Uneasy Troika in US Refugee Policy: Foreign Policy, Pressure Groups, and Resettlement Costs," *Journal of Refugee Studies,* Vol. 2, No. 3 (1989), pp. 364–71.

36. Zucker and Zucker, "The Uneasy Troika in US Refugee Policy," pp. 370–71; *New York Times,* September 29, 1988, p. 1; February 2, 1989, p. 4.

37. HIAS (Hebrew Immigrant Aid Society), Action Report, New York: April 1989.

38. *Refugee Reports,* Vol. 10, No. 6 (June 16, 1989), p. 1.

39. *Refugee Reports,* Vol. 12, No. 8 (August 30, 1991), p. 10.

40. *Refugee Reports,* Vol 15, No. 12 (December 31, 1994), p. 11.

41. *New York Times,* September 21, 1994, p. 3.

42. *Refugee Reports,* Vol. 15, No. 10 (October 27, 1994), p. 13.

43. Gail Paradise Kelly, *From Vietnam to America: A Chronicle of the Vietnamese Immigration to the United States* (Boulder, CO: Westview Press, 1977), p. 18.

44. Zucker and Zucker, *The Guarded Gate,* p. 44; Kelly, *From Vietnam to America.*

45. Robert L. Funseth, "Orderly Departure of Refugees from Vietnam," Current Policy No. 1199 (Washington, DC: US Department of State, Bureau of Public Affairs, 1989), p. 1.

46. Loescher and Scanlan, *Calculated Kindness,* p. 133.

47. US Department of Health and Human Services, Office of Refugee Resettlement, *Report to Congress, FY 1994, Refugee Resettlement Program,* p. 42.

48. *Report to Congress, FY 1994, Refugee Resettlement Program,* p. 51.

49. *New York Times,* July 12, 1995, p. 1; July 21, 1995, p. 6.

50. *Refugee Reports,* Vol. 16, No. 8 (August 25, 1995), p. 16; National Council of the Churches of Christ in the USA, Church World Service Immigration and Refugee Program, New York, *Monday,* Vol. 14, No. 14 (October 23, 1995), p. 2.

51. US Congress, House of Representatives. *The Refugee Act of 1979,* Report No. 96–608, 96th Congress, 1st Session (Washington, DC: US Government Printing Office, 1979), p. 13; Norman L. Zucker and Naomi Flink Zucker, "From Immigration to Refugee Redefinition: A History of Refugee and Asylum Policy in the United States," in Gil Loescher, ed., *Refugees and the Asylum Dilemma in the West* (University Park, PA: Pennsylvania State University Press, 1992), p. 63.

52. Ralston Deffenbaugh, "Resettlement as Protection: New Directions in the US Refugee Program," *Refugee Reports,* Vol. 15, No. 4 (April 24, 1994), pp. 10–12.

Notes for Chapter 3

1. *New York Times,* May 13, 1980, p. 14.

2. *New York Times,* December 14, 1980, p. 29.

3. Letter dated January 1, 1979.

4. Julia Vadala Taft, David S. North, and David A. Ford, *Refugee Resettlement in the US: Time for a New Focus* (Washington, DC: New TransCentury Foundation, July 31, 1979), p. 79.

5. Quoted in Félix Roberto Masud-Piloto, *With Open Arms: Cuban Migration to the United States* (Totowa, NJ: Rowman and Littlefield, 1988), p. 63.

6. *New York Times,* November 19, 1978, p. 13.

7. US Congress, Senate, Committee on the Judiciary, *Caribbean Refugee Crisis: Cubans and Haitians,* 96th Cong., 2nd Sess., May 12, 1980 (Washington, DC: US Government Printing Office, 1980), p. 23.

8. *Miami Herald,* October 5, 1982, p. 11A.

9. Robert L. Bach, "Cubans," in David W. Haines, ed., *Refugees in the United States: A Reference Handbook* (Westport, CT: Greenwood Press, 1985), p. 84.

10. *Miami Herald,* October 5, 1982, p. 11A.

11. *The Cuban Emigres: Was There a US Intelligence Failure?* Staff Report, Subcommittee on Oversight, Permanent Select Committee on Intelligence, US House of Representatives (Washington, DC: US Government Printing Office, 1980), p. 3.

12. *The Cuban Emigres: Was There a US Intelligence Failure?* p. 2.

13. *The Cuban Emigres: Was There a US Intelligence Failure?* p. 3.

14. Ronald Copeland, "The 1980 Cuban Crisis: Some Observations," *Journal of Refugee Resettlement,* August 1981, Vol. 1, No. 4, p. 23.

15. *New York Times,* April 9, 1980, p. 26.

16. *Chicago Tribune,* April 20, 1980, Sect. 2, p. 4.

17. *New York Times,* April 10, 1980, p. 1.

18. *New York Times,* April 24, 1980, p. 17.

19. See Gil Loescher and John A. Scanlan, *Calculated Kindness: Refugees and America's Half Open Door, 1945–Present* (New York: Free Press, 1986).

20. Loescher and John A. Scanlan, *Calculated Kindness,* pp. 181–82.

21. *Washington Post,* April 25, 1980, p. 1.

22. Statement by Elizabeth Holtzman, chair, House Subcommittee on Immigration, Refugees, and International Law, US House of Representatives, Washington, DC, June 17, 1980.

23. Ronald Copeland, "The Cuban Boatlift of 1980: Strategies in Federal Crisis Management," in Gilburt D. Loescher and John A. Scanlan, eds., *The Global Refugee*

Problem: US and World Response, The Annals of the American Academy of Political and Social Science, Vol. 467 (May 1983), p. 146.

24. *Washington Post,* May 6, 1980, p. 1A.

25. Current Policy No. 183 (Washington, DC: US Department of State, Bureau of Public Affairs, May 14, 1980).

26. *New York Times,* May 21, 1980, p. 24.

27. *Miami News,* May 7, 1980, p. 1.

28. *Washington Post,* May 4, 1980, p. 1.

29. *Miami Herald,* June 15, 1980, p. 1.

30. Copeland, "The Cuban Boatlift of 1980," p. 143.

31. *Washington Post,* May 4, 1980, p. 1.

32. *Miami Herald,* June 16, 1980, p. 1.

33. *Miami Herald,* June 27, 1980, p. 6A.

34. Cartoon signed by Timenees, *Oakland Tribune,* September 25, 1980, p. A19.

35. Statement by Elizabeth Holtzman, chair, House Subcommittee on Immigration, Refugees, and International Law, May 13, 1980.

36. *Congressional Record—Senate,* June 6, 1980, S. 6436.

37. *Congressional Quarterly,* Special Report: Refugees, "Cuban Refugee Crisis May Prompt Introduction of Special Legislation," Washington, DC, May 31, 1980, p. 1497.

38. *New York Times,* May 4, 1980, p. 1.

39. *Miami Herald,* May 8, 1980, p. 1.

40. Mario Antonio Rivera, *Decision and Structure: US Refugee Policy in the Mariel Crisis* (Lanham, MD: University Press of America, 1991), p. 96.

41. *St. Paul* [Minnesota] *Pioneer Press,* May 29, 1980.

42. *Philadelphia Daily News,* May 15, 1980.

43. *Washington Post,* May 2, 1980, p. A1.

44. *New York Times,* May 18, 1980, p. 32.

45. *Washington Star,* June 27, 1980, Section A., p. 4.

46. *Arkansas Democrat,* May 9, 1980.

47. *Dallas Morning News,* October 11, 1980, p. 1A.

48. *Wichita Eagle,* June 5, 1980, p. 2C.

49. *Phoenix Gazette,* June 4, 1980.

50. *Philadelphia Bulletin,* May 14, 1980, p. E5.

51. *Harrisburg* [Pennsylvania] *Evening News,* June 13, 1980, p. A1.

52. *Dallas Morning News,* October 12, 1980, p. 37A.

53. *Chicago Tribune,* June 16, 1980.

54. *New York Times,* May 21, 1980, p. 34.

55. *New York Times,* May 10, 1980, p. 1.

56. *Dallas Morning News,* October 17, 1980.

57. *Washington Post,* May 28, 1980, p. 18.

58. *Miami Herald,* December 3, 1980, p. 14A.

Notes for Chapter 4

1. Notes of meeting, August 16, 1978.

2. *Haitian Refugee Center v. Civiletti,* Final Order Granting Relief, July 2, 1980, p. 162.

3. Statement by Mike Trominski to the *New York Times,* reprinted in the *Charlotte Observer,* September 28, 1981, p. 9A.

4. Mark Gibney and Michael Stohl, "Human Rights and US Refugee Policy," in Mark Gibney, ed., *Open Borders? Closed Societies? The Ethical and Political Issues* (New York: Greenwood Press, 1988), p. 163.

5. Gibney and Stohl, "Human Rights and US Refugee Policy," p. 163.

6. Gibney and Stohl, "Human Rights and US Refugee Policy," p. 166.

7. *Refugee Reports,* Vol. 14, No. 3 (March 31, 1993), pp. 8–9.

8. "Haitian Migration to the US," Current Policy No. 191 (Washington, DC: US Department of State, Bureau of Public Affairs, June 17, 1980), p. 1.

9. "Haitian Migration to the US," p. 1.

10. INS, unpublished tabulations.

11. INS, internal memorandum, July 17, 1978.

12. Interview with attorney Steven Forester, September 1, 1981.

13. Temporary restraining order issued by US District Judge James Lawrence King, January 1979.

14. *Haitian Refugee Center v. Civiletti,* p. 1587.

15. *Haitian Refugee Center v. Civiletti,* Final Order Granting Relief, July 2, 1980, p. 451.

16. *Haitian Refugee Center v. Civiletti,* Final Order, p. 162.

17. "Text of Reagan's Speech Accepting the Republican Nomination," *New York Times,* July 18, 1980, p. 8.

18. H. Eugene Douglas, "The Problem of Refugees in a Strategic Perspective," *Strategic Review* (Fall 1982), p. 20.

19. Douglas, "The Problem of Refugees," p. 20.

20. *United States as a Country of Mass First Asylum,* Hearing, Subcommittee on Immigration and Refugee Policy, Committee on the Judiciary, US Senate, 97th Congress, 1st Session, July 31, 1981, p. 3.

21. Issue Paper, mimeo, no date, p. 1.

22. Issue Paper, no date, p. 2.

23. See Ira J. Kurzban and Deborah Anker, "The Haitian Saga," *Immigration Newsletter,* November–December 1982, Vol. 11, No. 6; see also Ira Kurzban, "The Haitian Case," in *Rights,* Vol. 28, No. 2 (June 1982).

24. Issue Paper, no date, p. 6.

25. Kurzban, "The Haitian Case," p. 6.

26. Kurzban, "The Haitian Case," p. 6.

27. US General Accounting Office, *Detention Policies Affecting Haitian Nationals* (Washington, DC: June 16, 1983), p. 17.

28. Remarks of Judge Alcee Hastings, Federal District Court, Miami, FL, September 2, 1981.

29. *Federal Register,* Vol. 47, No. 132 (July 9, 1982), p. 30044.

30. Issue Paper, no date, p. 5.

31. Article 33.

32. Issue Paper, no date, p. 5.

33. *Washington Post,* July 15, 1984, p. B7.

34. *Miami Herald,* July 3, 1981, p. 2C.

35. Agreement Between the United States of America and Haiti, Effected by Exchange of Notes, Signed at Port-au-Prince, September 23, 1981.

36. US Congress, House of Representatives, Committee on the Judiciary, Subcommittee on Immigration, Refugees, and International Law, *Immigration Reform, Hearings,* 97th Congress, 1st Session (October 28, 1981), statement by Alan C. Nelson, deputy commissioner, INS, p. 580.

37. *Miami Herald,* October 8, 1981, p. 16A.

38. *Miami News,* October 27, 1981, p. 4A.
39. *Miami News,* October 3, 1981, p. 14A.
40. *Miami Herald,* October 2, 1981, p. 6A.
41. *New York Times,* October 1, 1981, p. 34.
42. "A Proposal to Establish a Temporary Refuge Scheme in the Caribbean Region for Refugee and Migration Emergencies," *Special Report,* December 1995, Forced Migration Projects, Open Society Institute, New York.
43. Lawyers Committee for Human Rights, *Refugee Refoulement: The Forced Return of Haitians Under the US–Haitian Interdiction Agreement,* March 1990, pp. 35–37.
44. Lawyers Committee for Human Rights, pp. 37–38.
45. Lawyers Committee for Human Rights, pp. 38–39.
46. Immigration Task Force, memorandum, May 19, 1981.

Notes for Chapter 5

1. Cecilia Menjívar, "History, Economy and Politics: Macro and Micro-level Factors in Recent Salvadorean Migration to the US, *Journal of Refugee Studies,* Vol. 6, No. 4 (1993), p. 351.
2. Menjívar, "History, Economy and Politics," pp. 360–61.
3. Christopher Mitchell, "Introduction: Immigration and US Foreign Policy toward the Caribbean, Central America, and Mexico," in Christopher Mitchell, ed., *Western Hemisphere Immigration and United States Foreign Policy* (University Park, PA: Pennsylvania State University Press, 1992), p. 2.
4. President Ronald Reagan, "Strategic Importance of El Salvador and Central America," Current Policy No. 464 (Washington, DC: US Department of State, Bureau of Public Affairs, March 10, 1983).
5. See Gil Loescher and John A. Scanlan, *Calculated Kindness: Refugees and America's Half Open Door, 1945–Present* (New York: Free Press, 1986), p. 192; for a discussion of the Reagan administration refugee policy, see Chapter 10, "Reagan and the Closing Door."
6. Speech before a Republican fund-raising dinner, Jackson, Mississippi, June 20, 1983.
7. *New York Times,* February 23, 1982, p. 1.
8. Secretary Schultz, "Struggle for Democracy in Central America," Current Policy No. 478 (Washington, DC: US Department of State, Bureau of Public Affairs, April 15, 1983).
9. President Ronald Reagan, "Caribbean Basin Initiative," Current Policy No. 370 (Washington, DC: US Department of State, Bureau of Public Affairs, February 24, 1982).
10. *New York Times,* August 15, 1983, p. B6.
11. US Congress, Senate, Committee on the Judiciary, *Annual Refugee Consultation for 1982, Hearing,* 97th Congress, 1st Session, September 22, 1981, pp. 26–27.
12. *Refugee Reports,* Vol. 14, No. 12 (Washington, DC: US Committee for Refugees, December 31, 1993), p. 10.
13. Lars Schoultz, "Central America and the Politicization of US Immigration Policy," in Christopher Mitchell, ed., *Western Hemisphere Immigration and United States Foreign Policy* (University Park, PA: Pennsylvania State University Press, 1992), p. 197.
14. *New York Times,* September 22, 1983, p. 3.
15. *Refugee Reports,* December 31, 1992, p. 12.
16. See Schoultz, "Central America and the Politicization of US Immigration Policy," pp. 165–66.

17. William Stanley, "Economic Migrants or Refugees from Violence? A Time Series Analysis of Salvadoran Migration to the United States, June 1985," in *Central American Refugees*, Hearing before the Subcommittee on Census and Population, Committee on Post Office and Civil Service, House of Representatives, 99th Congress, 1st Session, June 27, 1985.

18. Stanley, "Economic Migrants or Refugees from Violence?" pp. 48–49.

19. Stanley, "Economic Migrants or Refugees from Violence?" p. 70.

20. Segundo Montes, "Migration to the United States as an Index of the Intensifying Social and Political Crises in El Salvador." *Journal of Refugee Studies,* Vol. 1, No. 2, 1988, p. 111.

21. Leo R. Chávez, Estevan T. Flores, and Marta López-Garza, "Migrants and Settlers: A Comparison of Undocumented Mexicans and Central Americans in the United States," *Frontera Norte,* Vol. 1, No. 1 (January–June, 1989), p. 55.

22. Chávez et al., "Migrants and Settlers," Table 3.

23. Sharon Stanton Russell, "Migration Patterns of US Foreign Policy Interest," in Michael S. Teitelbaum and Myron Weiner, eds., *Threatened Peoples, Threatened Borders: World Migration and US Policy* (New York: W.W. Norton, 1995), p. 51.

24. INS, *Asylum Adjudications: An Evolving Concept for the Immigration and Naturalization Service* (Washington, DC: June 1982), p. 32.

25. INS, *Asylum Adjudications,* p. 53.

26. Gary MacEoin and Nivita Riley, *No Promised Land: American Refugee Policies and the Rule of Law* (Boston, MA: Oxfam America, 1982), p. 57.

27. *New York Times,* February 3, 1985, p. 30.

28. Helsinki Watch, *Detained, Denied, Deported: Asylum Seekers in the United States,* June 1989, p. 26.

29. Deborah E. Anker, Executive Summary, *Determining Asylum Claims in the United States: An Empirical Case Study,* Final Report, April 1991, p. 9.

30. INS, *Asylum Adjudications,* p. 59.

31. Helsinki Watch, *Detained, Denied, Deported,* p. 65.

32. *Central American Refugees*, Hearings, p. 119.

33. *Washington Post,* July 10, 1980, p. 10.

34. Gary MacEoin, "A Brief History of the Sanctuary Movement," in Gary MacEoin, ed., *Sanctuary: A Resource Guide* (San Francisco: Harper and Row, 1985), p. 18.

35. Interview with Jim Corbett, Tucson, Arizona, June 5, 1985.

36. Barbara M. Yarnold, *Refugees Without Refuge: Formation and Failed Implementation of US Political Asylum Policy in the 1980's* (Lanham, NY: University Press of America, 1990), p. 224.

37. Schoultz, "Central America and the Politicization of US Immigration Policy," pp. 210–11.

38. Schoultz, "Central America and the Politicization of US Immigration Policy," p. 190.

39. *Orantes-Hernandez v. Smith,* 541 F.Supp. 351 (C.D. Cal. 1982).

40. Quoted in *Interpreter Releases,* Vol. 59, No. 32 (August 25, 1982), p. 525.

41. *Refuge: Canada's Periodical on Refugees* (Center for Refugee Studies, York University, Ontario, Canada), Vol. 7, No. 1, September 1987.

42. *Interpreter Releases,* Vol. 59, No. 18, May 6, 1982.

43. *Extended Voluntary Departure Issues,* Hearing before the Subcommittee on Immigration and Refugee Policy, Committee on the Judiciary, US Senate, 99th Congress, 1st Session, April 22, 1985, pp. 76–77.

44. *Extended Voluntary Departure Issues,* p. 89.

45. Letter to the Congress, July 31, 1985.

46. *Extended Voluntary Departure Issues,* p. 59.

47. Letter to Senator DeConcini and Representative Moakley, in *Extended Voluntary Departure Issues,* p. 76.

48. *New York Times,* May 12, 1987, p. 30.

49. *New York Times,* September 11, 1988, p. 9.

50. *New York Times,* March 30, 1986, p. 1.

51. *New York Times,* April 17, 1986, p. 1.

52. US Department of Justice, Press Release, July 8, 1987.

53. Correspondence from Ralph Thomas, Immigration and Naturalization Service, October 1, 1987.

54. US District Court of California, in *Orantes-Hernandez v. Meese and INS,* CV 82–1107 KN, April 1988.

55. *Refugee Reports,* Vol. 9, No. 5 (May 20, 1988), p. 9.

56. *Nuñez v. Boldin,* 557 F. Supp. 578 (S.D. Tex. 1982).

57. Memorandum to Francis A. Keating II, Acting Associate Attorney General, from the Office of the Commissioner, INS, October 3, 1988.

58. The US Committee for Refugees, Issue Brief, *Refugees at Our Border: The US Response to Asylum Seekers* (Washington, DC: September 1989), pp. 1–2.

59. Memorandum from Francis A. Keating, Acting Associate Attorney General, to Alan C. Nelson, Commissioner, INS, December 2, 1988.

60. US Committee for Refugees, Issue Brief, *Refugees at Our Border,* p. 3.

61. US Committee for Refugees, *Refugees at Our Border,* p. 3.

62. US Committee for Refugees, *Refugees at Our Border,* p. 4.

63. US Committee for Refugees, *Refugees at Our Border,* pp. 5–6.

64. US Committee for Refugees, *Refugees at Our Border,* pp. 6–7.

65. US Committee for Refugees, *Refugees at Our Border,* p. 7.

66. Paula Pearlman, "Litigation to Stop I.N.S. Abuse of Salvadoran Asylum Seeker," *Refuge,* Vol. 7, No. 1 (September 1987), p. 7.

67. *Refugee Reports,* Vol. 10, No. 5 (May 19, 1989).

68. *Refugee Reports,* Vol. 12, No. 1 (January 29, 1991), p. 2.

69. Memo from James L. Buck, deputy commissioner, INS, December 5, 1988.

70. US Committee for Refugees, Issue Paper, *Running the Gauntlet: The Central American Journey through Mexico* (Washington, DC: 1991), p. 4.

71. US Committee for Refugees, *Running the Gauntlet,* pp. 4–6.

72. Anker, Executive Summary, *Determining Asylum Claims,* p. 2.

73. Gregg A. Beyer, "Establishing the United States Asylum Officer Corps: A First Report," *International Journal of Refugee Law,* Vol. 4, No. 4 (1992).

74. Beyer, "Establishing the United States Asylum Officer Corps," p. 463, fn. 63.

75. Beyer, "Establishing the United States Asylum Officer Corps," p. 464.

76. Beyer, "Establishing the United States Asylum Officer Corps," pp. 474–75.

77. *Refugee Reports,* Vol. 13, No. 12 (December 31, 1992), p. 12.

78. *New York Times,* January 5, 1996, p. 10.

79. Sarah Ignatius, *An Assessment of the Asylum Process of the Immigration and Naturalization Service,* National Asylum Study Project, Immigration and Refugee Progam, Harvard Law School, Cambridge, MA, September 1993, p. 1.

80. Ignatius, *An Assessment of the Asylum Process,* p. 4.

Notes for Chapter 6

1. Executive Office of the Governor and Florida Advisory Council on Intergovernmental Relations, "The Unfair Burden: Immigration's Impact on Florida" (Tallahassee, FL: March 1994).

2. *Newsweek,* August 9, 1993, pp. 18–19.

3. *New York Times,* June 27, 1993, p. 1.

4. *New York Times,* September 21, 1994, p. 21.

5. *New York Times,* January 20, 1994, Section 4, p. 1.

6. *New York Times,* December 27, 1995, p. 1.

7. Palmer Stacy and Wayne Lutton, *The Immigration Time Bomb* (Monterey, VA: The American Immigration Control Foundation, 1988), p. 41.

8. *New York Times,* October 15, 1993, p. 34.

9. Michael S. Teitelbaum and Myron Weiner, "Introduction: Threatened Peoples, Threatened Borders, Migration and US Foreign Policy," in Michael S. Teitelbaum and Myron Weiner, eds., *Threatened Peoples, Threatened Borders: World Migration and US Policy* (New York: W.W. Norton, 1995), p. 29.

10. US Commission on Immigration Reform, Executive Summary, *US Immigration Policy: Restoring Credibility, A Report to Congress* (Washington, DC: 1994), p. 29.

11. Alex Stepick, "Unintended Consequences: Rejecting Haitian Boat People and Destabilizing Duvalier," in Christopher Mitchell, ed., *Western Hemisphere Immigration and United States Foreign Policy* (University Park, PA: Pennsylvania State University Press, 1992), p. 127.

12. Americas Watch, The National Coalition for Haitian Refugees and Caribbean Rights, *Haiti: The Aristide Government's Human Rights Record: A Report,* Vol. 3, No. 12 (November 1, 1991), p. 7.

13. *Haiti Insight,* Vol. 2, No. 8 (February 1991), p. 1.

14. Americas Watch, *Haiti: The Aristide Government's Human Rights Record,* passim; *Haiti Insight,* Vol. 3, No. 1 (May 1991), p. 1.

15. *Haiti Insight,* Vol. 3, No. 5 (October 1991), p. 1.

16. Cheryl Little, "United States Haitian Policy: A History of Discrimination," *New York Law School Journal of Human Rights,* Vol. 10, Part 2 (Spring 1993), p. 298.

17. Open Society Institute, Special Report, *A Proposal to Establish a Temporary Refuge Scheme in the Caribbean Region for Refugee and Migration Emergencies* (December 1995), p. 3.

18. *Haiti Insight,* Vol. 3, No. 7 (March/April 1992), p. 1.

19. National Council of the Churches of Christ in the USA, New York, *Report of the NCC/CCLA Delegation to Haiti* (August 27–September 1, 1992), p. 4.

20. *New York Times,* February 5, 1992, p. 8.

21. *Washington Post,* May 27, 1992, p. 24.

22. *Washington Post,* June 1, 1992, p. 19A.

23. *Refugee Reports,* Vol. 15, No. 2 (February 28, 1994), p. 12.

24. *Washington Post,* May 23, 1992, p. 1.

25. *Haiti Insight,* Vol. 4, No. 1 (May/June 1992), p. 1.

26. *New York Times,* May 28, 1992, p. 3.

27. Clinton Statement on Appeals Court Ruling on Haitian Repatriation, US Newswire, May 27, 1992, available in LEXIS, Nexis Library, Current File; *New York Times,* May 27, 1992, p. 1.

28. *New York Times,* May 25, 1992, p. 1.

29. Amnesty International USA, *Amnesty Action* (Summer/Fall 1992), p. 8.

30. *Washington Post,* May 27, 1992, p. A24.

31. *The Economist,* November 28, 1992, p. 26.

32. National Council of the Churches of Christ in the USA, Church World Service Immigration and Refugee Program, New York, *Monday,* Vol. 12, No. 1 (January 4, 1993), pp. 1–2; photocopy of letter sent by the National Coalition for Haitian Refugees to President-elect Bill Clinton, December 1, 1992.

33. Doris M. Meissner, Dear Colleague Letter, December 10, 1992.

34. *New York Times,* December 31, 1992, p. 1.

35. *Washington Post,* November 12, 1992, p. A1.

36. *New York Times,* January 17, 1993, Section 4, p. 16.

37. *Refugee Reports,* Vol. 14, No. 1 (January 29, 1993), p. 1.

38. American Immigration Lawyers Association (AILA), *Human Rights Delegation Report on Haiti,* Washington, DC, March 1993, p. 1.

39. National Council of the Churches of Christ in the USA, *Report of the NCC/CCLA Delegation to Haiti,* p. 2.

40. Americas Watch, National Coalition for Haitian Refugees, Jesuit Refugee Service/USA, *No Port in a Storm: The Misguided Use of In-Country Refugee Processing in Haiti,* Vol. 5, Issue 8 (September 1993), pp. 7–30.

41. US Committee for Refugees, *World Refugee Survey: 1995* (Washington, DC, 1995), pp. 180–181; *Refugee Reports,* Vol. 15, No. 5 (May 31, 1994), pp. 1–2.

42. Statement of President-elect Bill Clinton on the Crisis in Haiti, January 14, 1993.

43. Harold Hongju Koh, "The 'Haiti Paradigm' in United States Human Rights Policy," *Yale Law Journal,* Vol. 103 (1994), p. 2396.

44. Affidavit of Louis Henkin, December 15, 1992, p. 3, in *Gene McNary, Commissioner, Immigration and Naturalization Service, et al. v. Haitian Centers Council, Inc. et al.* (No. 92–344, Supreme Court of the United States, October Term, 1992).

45. Harold Hongju Koh, "Reflections on Refoulement and Haitian Centers Council," *Harvard International Law Journal,* Vol. 35, No. 1 (Winter 1994), p. 11.

46. *Refugee Reports,* Vol. 14, No. 6 (June 30, 1993), p. 2.

47. Koh, "Reflections," p. 18.

48. UNHCR, Statement: "Office of the High Commissioner Concerned by Supreme Court Haitian Decision," Washington, DC, June 22, 1993.

49. *New York Times,* October 12, 1993, p. 1.

50. *New York Times,* December 8, 1995, p. 30.

51. *New York Times,* July 6, 1994, p. 1.

52. Human Rights Watch, *Human Rights Watch World Report 1995: Events of 1994* (New York: Human Rights Watch, 1995), p. 102.

53. US Department of State, "Human Rights in Haiti," third interim report, Washington, DC, September 13, 1994, p. 1.

54. Transcript of President Clinton's Address to the Nation, *New York Times,* September 16, 1994, p. 10.

55. *New York Times,* October 14, 1994, p. 1.

56. *Haiti Insight,* Vol. 6, No. 1 (October–November 1995), p. 7.

57. Human Rights Watch, *Human Rights Watch World Report 1996: Events of 1995* (New York: Human Rights Watch, 1996), p. 103.

58. *New York Times,* April 18, 1996, p. A14.

59. Department of State and Department of Defense, *The Soviet-Cuban Connection in Central America and the Caribbean,* Washington, DC, March 1985, p. 3.

60. Human Rights Watch, *World Report 1994,* p. 89.

61. Human Rights Watch, *World Report 1994,* p. 89; *New York Times,* January 14, 1992, p. 10.

62. Julia A. Spinthourakis, Sally J. Moore, and Catherine M. Duncan, *Florida's Refugee Fact Book: 1994* (Tallahassee, FL: Florida Department of Health and Rehabilitative Services, September 29, 1994), p. 59.

63. *New York Times,* May 8, 1995, p. 1.

64. Kathleen Newland, "The Impact of US Refugee Policies on US Foreign Policy:

A Case of the Tail Wagging the Dog?" in Michael S. Teitelbaum and Myron Weiner, eds., *Threatened Peoples, Threatened Borders: World Migration and US Policy* (New York: W.W. Norton, 1995), p. 205.

65. Carla Anne Robbins, "Dateline Washington: Cuban-American Clout," *Foreign Policy*, No. 88 (Fall 1992), p. 163.

66. Gillian Gunn, *Cuba in Transition: Options for US Policy* (New York: Twentieth Century Fund Press, 1993), p. 21.

67. Gunn, *Cuba in Transition*, pp. 21–22.

68. Gunn, *Cuba in Transition*, p. 26.

69. Human Rights Watch/Americas Watch, *Cuba: Repression, the Exodus of August 1994 and the US Response*, Vol. 6, No. 12 (October 1994), p. 6.

70. Human Rights Watch/Americas Watch, *Cuba: Repression*, p. 8.

71. Human Rights Watch, *World Report 1995*, p. 85.

72. Human Rights Watch/Americas Watch, *Cuba: Repression*, p. 5.

73. *New York Times*, August 7, 1994, p. 17.

74. *New York Times*, August 11, 1994, p. 22.

75. Human Rights Watch/Americas Watch, *Cuba: Repression*, pp. 86–87; US Committee for Refugees, *World Refugee Survey 1995*, pp. 176–77.

76. Spinthourakis et al., *Florida's Refugee Fact Book*, p. 60.

77. *New York Times*, August 19, 1994, p. 14.

78. *New York Times*, July 5, 1993, p. 4.

79. *New York Times*, August 14, 1994, p. 20.

80. *New York Times*, August 25, 1994, p. 14.

81. *New York Times*, October 6, 1993, p. 1; May 16, 1994, p. 16; August 31, 1994, p. 11.

82. Excerpts from News Conference announcement, *New York Times*, August 19, 1994, p. 12.

83. Excerpts from News Conference.

84. Open Society Institute, *A Proposal to Establish a Temporary Refuge*, p. 5.

85. Human Rights Watch/Americas Watch, *Cuba: Repression*, pp. 10–11.

86. Text of the Joint Communique issued by the United States and Cuba in New York on September 9, 1994, reprinted in *Migration World*, Vol. 23, No. 5, p. 13.

87. *Refugee Reports*, Vol. 15, No. 9 (September 19, 1994), p. 6.

88. *Refugee Reports*, Vol. 15, No. 9 (September 19, 1994), p. 7.

89. Human Rights Watch/Americas Watch, *Cuba: Repression*, p. 13.

90. Human Rights Watch/Americas Watch, *Cuba: Repression*, pp. 12–13.

91. *New York Times*, October 26, 1994, p. 18.

92. *Cuban American Bar Association v. Christopher*, 43F. 3d 1412 (11th Cir. 1995); *Haitian Refugee Center v. Christopher*, 43F. 3d (11th Cir. 1995).

93. Bill Frelick, "Safe Haven: Safe for Whom?" in *World Refugee Survey, 1995* (Washington, DC: US Committee for Refugees, 1995), p. 18.

94. US General Accounting Office, *Cuba: US Response to the 1994 Cuban Migration Crisis* (Washington, DC: September 1995), p. 4; *Refugee Reports*, Vol. 16, No. 9 (September 29, 1995), p. 3.

95. *New York Times*, May 21, 1995, p. 8; *Refugee Reports*, Vol. 16, No. 9 (September 1995), pp. 3, 13.

96. *New York Times*, May 5, 1995, p. 1.

97. *Refugee Reports*, Vol. 16, No. 9 (September 1995), pp. 13–14.

98. *New York Times*, October 6, 1995, p. 10.

99. *New York Times*, February 1, 1996, p. 8.

Notes for Chapter 7

1. For a discussion of the problem of durable solutions, see Gil Loescher, *Beyond Charity: International Cooperation and the Global Refugee Crisis* (New York: Oxford University Press, 1993), pp. 148–50.

2. UNHCR, *The State of the World's Refugees: In Search of Solutions* (New York: Oxford University Press, 1995), p. 35.

3. David A. Martin, "Strategies for a Resistant World: Human Rights Initiatives and the Need for Alternatives to Refugee Interdiction," *Cornell International Law Journal,* Vol. 26 (1993), p. 754.

4. UNHCR, *The State of the World's Refugees,* pp. 46–47.

5. Resolution 698 (1991): UN Security Council, S/RES/688 (1991). For a full discussion, see Bill Frelick, " 'Preventive Protection' and the Right to Seek Asylum: A Preliminary Look at Bosnia and Croatia," *International Journal of Refugee Law,* Vol. 4, No. 4 (1992), pp. 439–40.

6. Quoted in Bill Frelick, " 'Preventive Protection,' " p. 443.

7. UNHCR, *The State of the World's Refugees,* p. 147.

8. UNHCR, *The State of the World's Refugees,* pp. 147–48.

9. Aristide R. Zolberg, Astri Suhrke, and Sergio Aguayo, *Escape from Violence: Conflict and the Refugee Crisis in the Developing World* (New York: Oxford University Press, 1989), p. 260.

10. UNHCR, *The State of the World's Refugees,* p. 153.

11. Gil Loescher, "The International Refugee Regime: Stretched to the Limit?" *Journal of International Affairs,* Vol. 47, No. 2 (Winter 1994), p. 376.

12. Commission on Global Governance, *Our Global Neighborhood* (New York: Oxford University Press, 1995), p. 71.

13. Organization of African Unity Convention Governing the Specific Aspects of Refugee Problems in Africa, Article 1, Point 2 (Addis Ababa, Ethiopia: September 10, 1969).

14. Cartagena Declaration on Refugees (Cartagena, Chile: 1984), Section III, Article 3.

15. Forced Migration Projects, *A Proposal to Establish a Temporary Refuge Scheme in the Caribbean Region for Refugee and Migration Emergencies,* Special Report (New York, NY: Open Society Institute, December 1995), p. 6. See also Dennis Gallagher, Susan Forbes, and Patricia Weiss Fagen, *Safe Haven: Policy Responses to Refugee-Like Situations* (Washington, DC: Refugee Policy Group, June 1987).

16. Harold Hongju Koh, "The 'Haiti Paradigm' in United States Human Rights Policy," *Yale Law Journal,* Vol. 103, p. 2431, fn. 221.

17. *New York Times,* January 15, 1996, p. 3.

18. Quoted in Forced Migration Projects, *A Proposal to Establish a Temporary Refuge Scheme,* p. 3.

19. Kathleen Newland, *US Refugee Policy: Dilemmas and Directions* (Washington, DC: Carnegie Endowment for International Peace, 1995), p. 17.

20. Kathleen Newland, *US Refugee Policy,* pp. 17–18.

21. See *New York Times,* January 3, 1996, p. 8.

22. *New York Times,* December 1, 1995, p. 1.

23. David A. Martin, "Making Asylum Policy: The 1994 Reforms," *Washington Law Review,* Vol. 70, No. 715 (1995), p. 740.

24. UNHCR, *The State of the World's Refugees,* p. 197.

25. Carl Kaysen, "Refugees: Concepts, Norms, Realities, and What the United States Can and Should Do," in Michael S. Teitelbaum and Myron Weiner, eds., *Threatened Peoples, Threatened Borders: World Migration and US Policy* (New York: W.W. Norton, 1995), pp. 248–49.

26. Atle Grahl-Madsen, *Territorial Asylum* (Upsala: Swedish Insititute of International Law, 1978), p. vii.

Index

About the Authors

Norman L. Zucker and **Naomi Flink Zucker** live in Kingston, Rhode Island. They have been studying and writing on American refugee policy for many years. Their last book was *The Guarded Gate: The Reality of American Refugee Policy,* which was named an outstanding book on the subject of intolerance by the Gustavus Myers Center.